The Way of the Wave

Also by Daniel A. Miller

Losing Control, Finding Serenity: How the Need to Control Hurts Us and How to Let It Go

The Gifts of Acceptance: Embracing People and Things as They Are

Acceptance in the Time of COVID-19
(a free guide at danielamiller.com)

How to Invest in Real Estate Syndicates

Praise for *The Gifts of Acceptance*

"Best-selling author Miller learned the hard way that his control-driven lifestyle wasn't working and that only by letting go of the reins would he find more tranquility . . . to accept life on life's terms . . . to welcome what is instead of what one hopes the world to be. VERDICT: A solid reminder to enjoy the life we've been given. Highly recommended."
—*Library Journal* Starred Review and
Best Wellness Book of the Year

"[The book] uses case histories and author experiences to illustrate the predicament and the contrast between controlling and accepting behavior patterns. The result is an informational title packed with strategies, tools, and tips for negotiating ups and downs with a new paradigm for living a better life."
—D. Donovan, Senior Reviewer, *Midwest Book Review*

"Danny has written a masterpiece on the art and science of acceptance, revealing the paradoxical relationship between true acceptance and transformation—the key to serenity, vitality, clarity, love, joy, and wisdom."
—Joseph Bailey, author of *The Serenity Principle* and
Slowing Down to the Speed of Life

"Miller's book is absolutely key to understanding acceptance and how to flourish within the confines of relationships that snag our ego. I highly recommend this book to those who struggle to simply 'let people be.'"
—Karen Casey, PhD, bestselling author of *Let Go Now*

"This is a must read for the entire family. Benefit from it and refer back to it often as life goes on."
—*Keys to Recovery Newspaper*

"Strategies and tools are provided to help readers overcome [specific situations and obstacles]. . . . It is never too late to change being stuck permanently in the life you have now . . . and adopt some or all of the tools Miller provides in his book."
—Norm Goldman, Publisher, Bookpleasures.com

Praise for *Losing Control, Finding Serenity*

"Daniel A. Miller has done an amazing job in delving deeply into the crevices of how most of us need to be in control. He has created a way of guiding and educating the reader, in a very understandable and logical way, to help everyone 'Let Go.' A must read for everyone!"

—*In Light Times*

"Down-to-earth and honest, the book is full of psychological and spiritual insight. It is also full of real world solutions for reconnecting with the natural flow of life and with our personal truth."

—*New Age Retailer*

"Reading Miller's words really helped me to understand the many ways control plays a part in my life—and he offered some great advice on how to let go of the need for control."

—Dani DiPirro, *Positively Present*

"*Losing Control, Finding Serenity* pinpoints the dangers of excessive control. It shows those of us who feel the pressure to control how to break free and reap unexpected gifts. Drawing on psychological insights, spiritual wisdom, and the real-life stories of acknowledged control freaks, the author guides us through an honest inventory of our control patterns, leading us to discover this compulsion is provoked by deep-seated fear, anxiety, and insecurity, then aggravated by anger and resentments. In a chaotic, unpredictable world that's frequently beyond our control, *Losing Control, Finding Serenity* offers welcome encouragement and validation for going with the flow of life as it is: an ongoing, ever changing mystery."

—*The Monthly Aspectarian*

THE WAY OF THE WAVE

Nature's Model for Navigating Life's Currents

Daniel A. Miller

Ebb and Flow Press
Sherman Oaks, California

Published by
Ebb and Flow Press
13547 Ventura Blvd., # 93
Sherman Oaks, California 91423

Printed in the United States of America

Cover painting by Daniel A. Miller
Cover and text design by Mayapriya Long, Bookwrights

Cataloging-in-Publication data

Names: Miller, Daniel Aron, 1943-, author.
Title: The way of the wave : nature's model for navigating life's currents / Daniel A. Miller.
Description: Includes bibliographical references. | Sherman Oaks, CA: Ebb and Flow Press, 2025.
Identifiers: LCCN: 2024909989 | ISBN: 978-0-9828930-7-4 (paperback)
Subjects: LCSH Self-actualization (Psychology.) | Conduct of life. | Happiness. | Interpersonal relationships. | Self help. | BISAC SELF-HELP / Personal Growth / Happiness | MIND BODY & SPIRIT / Inspiration. | MIND BODY & SPIRIT / Personal Growth
Classification: LCC BF637.S4 .M55 2025 | 158.1--dc23 DDC

To my three dear children, Lana, Lora and Brandon,
who bring me great joy

Life's Lantern

Obsessed with control,
We can't let go.
And shorten life's List,
The more we resist.

Relinquish,
No longer diminish.
Let things be,
Start to feel free.

To travel this path,
Use its new math.
Accept and allow—
Even meow.

Look to the waves,
Follow their sways.
Cresting in the wind,
Nature's magic within.

Sometimes in tandem,
Always random.
Release,
Feel the Peace.

Life's rhythm of truth,
Lost in youth,
Follows no pattern, yet
Brightens life's lantern.

—Daniel A. Miller

Contents

The winds and the waves are always on the side of the ablest navigators.

—Edward Gibbon, *The History of the Decline and Fall of the Roman Empire*

It Began That Day
at the Beach

MY LIFE CHANGED FOREVER that day at the beach in Santa Monica over thirty-five years ago.

As I sat alone watching the waves rise and travel to shore, I became mesmerized by their infinite variety, randomness, unpredictability, and awesome power.

They had a wonderful freedom, naturalness, and mystery to them that comforted me. For the previous five years, I had been battered by what seemed like a never-ending barrage of personal and financial setbacks that shook me to my core. I was experiencing an unfamiliar relief, together with feelings of aloneness and unknowing about the future.

Many of my travails had been of my own doing. My unharnessed self-will had taken its toll—mentally, physically, financially, and spiritually. As a fear-driven controller, I didn't know how to relent, let alone pause—until I had to.

It culminated when I went into the hospital for what I was told would be a twenty-minute outpatient procedure to remove a skin cancer lesion on my right nostril. I had kept putting it off while dealing with my other struggles—the bank's calling loans (over $1 million in today's dollars) bringing me to the brink of bankruptcy coupled with a five-year legal battle with a business partner intent on squeezing me out of my most profitable real estate investment; a deranged neighbor setting fire to my garage directly beneath my eight-year-old son's bedroom; one of my office buildings burning down; robberies, murder, and loss of tenants at another; and a difficult divorce.

I ended up on the operating table for over three hours, followed by three major surgeries over a six-week period to eradicate the cancerous tissue that had spread through my face like the roots of a tree. I lost half my nose, and it took several more surgeries to reconstruct it. And to my remorse, my insurance coverage was dropped after the first round of surgeries.

Only then was I able to accept the folly of my control-driven life. I had neither the strength nor desire to go on fighting whatever demons were going to attack me next.

I surrendered.

The emotional scars were even deeper. I badly needed healing. That's what brought me to the beach that day.

Sitting on the rocks, I intuitively knew that the way of the waves held the keys to a better life for me. They were a metaphor for a vision of the life I was seeking: one with less stress, worry, and conflict and greater peace and serenity—and, unlike before, one in which I could meet whatever challenges that may lay ahead with acceptance, trust, and even grace.

Like waves, life is in a constant state of motion; it's fluid, shifting and always changing, sometimes quickly, sometimes smoothly, other times bumpily and abruptly. We can't control or predict what might happen at any given moment despite our best-laid plans and desires.

We may be having a peaceful morning at home or a productive day at work when something unexpected happens that puts us in a foul mood or churns our stomach. Conversely, we may be in a rut or feeling stuck, and something exciting pops up out of the blue that completely changes our mood.

I wanted to begin living my life as if I were riding waves and aligning with their currents rather than resisting and directing as I had always done. In short, like that popular expression, I wanted to "go with the flow" in dealing with important issues, relationships, and challenges in my life.

It felt good thinking or saying it, but I wondered, *How do you actually do it?* I didn't know. At times, I had glimpses while painting or playing tennis and experiencing the liberating feeling of being in the "zone," that state of grace when things seem to come to us almost effortlessly, rather than we to them, and where thoughts and ideas spring forth freely, almost magically. But those times were infrequent.

When I felt stressed, or anxious, or uncertain, I began saying to myself, "Go with the Wave; just go with the Wave." I also began thinking in the parlance of waves because it closely parallels what we experience in our lives: high and low tides, ebbs and flows, crests and swells, riptides and undertows, ripples and troughs, and such. These references served as visceral reminders for me to try to align with and be guided by the innate wisdom and rhythm of the natural world.

While these things helped, the benefits usually didn't last long. I was often thrown asunder by my strong judgments and high expectations, limited and negative

thinking, self-righteousness, avoidance and denial, failure to set boundaries, and excessive fear and anger.

I also was not mindful enough of the fact that my
wave was not the only wave in my personal universe and
that I needed to accept and honor the waves of others,
lest I find myself making waves!

Although I have made good progress in overcoming
these barriers to navigating my life currents, they remain
a constant, daily challenge for me. The difference now,
however, is that the misalignments are not as severe and
do not last as long because I have learned some effective
tools and strategies to counter them. Part 2 of the book
examines the impact of these obstructors more closely
and what you can do to overcome them.

Importantly, I have also learned how wave enhancers can facilitate the flow—ones such as acceptance,
trust, humility, truth, intuition, and self-care. Part 3 of
the book studies these enhancers and shows how they
are instrumental to going with the flow.

It has been an enlightening almost forty-year journey
of discovery, exploration, introspection, and practice—
marked with both success and failure—of trying to
go with the Wave in all aspects of my life: in love and
romance, parenting, interacting with friends and foes,
work and business, creative and sports endeavors, endur-
ing aging, dealing with a loved one's addiction, and facing
today's formidable tidal wave, our country's Great Divide.
Parts 4 and 5 of the book explore these life currents and
how the obstructors and enhancers impact them.

Along the way, my life has been enriched by many
unexpected and exciting moments. I have been blessed
to have ridden currents to destinations never before

reached, rewards never imagined, and soulful connections and inner peace never before felt.

I went from being a closed-minded, control-driven businessman to a more accepting, life-loving person who welcomes every day with gratitude and a prayer for acceptance and guidance instead of dread and foreboding.

I became a skilled artist (seascapes are my favorite subject) after not being able to draw (or so I believed) and an earnest poet after having been a droll writer. I have authored award-winning and best-selling personal-growth books, spoken extensively about control and acceptance dynamics, and written over 150 articles on those and related subjects for popular personal-growth blogs and at danielamiller.com.

I became a nationally ranked senior master's tennis player and learned not to judge my game and to trust my body's innate wisdom and ability. And most importantly, I met a beautiful (in all ways) woman who is my best friend and forever sweetheart and formed deeper bonds with my family and friends.

In the following chapters, I share personal stories and experiences that have educated me (sometimes painfully) about the ways of the Wave in different areas of my life as well as mindsets and practices that facilitate aligning with the flow and ones that hinder it.

At the end of each chapter, I offer some questions and prompts for you to reflect on that I hope will assist in delving deeper into the subjects discussed as they relate to your own life. I have found that a simple question or reflection can sometimes lead to an important revelation or insight.

Any guidance and suggestions are offered with a great deal of humility; you can choose what resonates with you and leave the rest. Riding the Wave remains a work in progress for me. Many times, I neglect or am not able to follow my own learnings, but when I do, my life is notably fuller.

As you face the challenges ahead, I encourage you to visualize ocean waves and their energy traveling to shore[1] or mountain streams flowing naturally, rhythmically, and freely; open yourself up to the innate wisdom of nature's magic within; and let it be your guide.

The way of the Wave has become a personal life philosophy and model to live by. For me, it is one of life's most beautiful poems—one that reduces fear, anxiety, worry, and self-imposed restrictions and limitations and lessens grief, loss, and hardship. It shines light on choices that manifestly improve my life and continues to bring more freedom, joy, and contentment than I ever could have imagined.

My hope is that it will be for you as well.

PART ONE

The Wave

CHAPTER ONE

The Wave

> When anxious, uneasy and bad thoughts come, I go to the sea, and the sea drowns them out with its great wide sounds, cleanses me with its noise, and imposes a rhythm upon everything in me that is bewildered and confused.
>
> —Rainer Maria Rilke

WHEN YOU OBSERVE NATURE for any period, you can sense the presence of a rhythmic process. You may notice it in the way autumn leaves fall from a tree, gently descending to form eloquent patterns on the grass, or in winter when soft snowflakes float gracefully in the air. You can sense it in the subtle movement and changing shapes of clouds in the sky, imbued with hues of light and dark. Or as I first did, watching the way ocean waves build, crest, and unfold in a boundless variety of ways.

This natural process and rhythm is not always benign. At times, we must endure powerful storms, piercing winds, perilous floods, shattering earth tremors, and such. In a similar manner, our lives are jolted by severe loss, trauma, and disease.

Whatever the moment we may be experiencing, we can sense an energy or life force that is unpredictable and unknowable, yet it seems to have an innate, vast intelligence all its own—one well beyond our capacity to understand. We can also sense that, as mysterious as this universal rhythm may be, we are somehow a part of it. There is a certain cohesiveness to it, a harmony of shared coexistence, a wisdom waiting to be revealed and learned.

I metaphorically refer to this rhythm or energy force as the Wave. It is intrinsically natural and truthful and cannot be controlled or manipulated. It just *is*, and though at times it feels ancient, it is always present and with us.

Ralph Waldo Emerson poetically described its essence:

"There is a guidance for each of us, and by lowly listening we shall hear the right word . . . Place yourself in the middle of the stream of power and wisdom which animates all whom it floats, and you are without effort impelled to truth, to right, and a perfect contentment."[1]

Before that day at the beach, I had no inkling of such a guidance and certainly no contentment. I had been engulfed in too many futile battles to notice.

Today, however, I feel the comfort of its presence as I walk out to my backyard in the early morning and listen to the cheerful medleys of songbirds and the cooing of doves, watch the branches of my magnificent olive tree with its glittering leaves reaching toward the day's young sky and with squirrels scampering about its strong limbs.

Indeed, I feel it in the stillness and solitude of nature most anywhere—when I hug an oak tree and am comforted by its grounding presence, inhale the medicinal aroma of eucalyptus leaves, delight in watching bright-colored hummingbirds darting from flower to flower, and of course when I become enthralled by the awesome power of waves when I am at the beach. I feel it, too, when I'm immersed in an evolving painting or channeling verses that occasionally lead to poems.

I have come to learn that the more I am able to align myself with this stream of power and wisdom, or ride the Wave, the more I discover solutions to my most pressing and troubling concerns and enjoy the unplanned, spontaneous moments in life. My spirit is lighter, and I am graced with greater peace and serenity.

In California, we have a long coastline with many beautiful beaches, and body-surfing the waves is a fun and popular activity and pastime. Body-surfing waves serves as a good analogy for the factors involved in navigating our life currents. The parallels are close.

While we are in the water, a variety of waves will constantly come in, some building quickly and crashing mightily, others cresting more gradually and lasting longer. Many unexpectedly change course. Some simply vanish.

We have no control over or influence on their patterns, paths, and frequencies; we can only be patient, observant, and alert as we wait for a wave that we intuitively sense is a good one to ride. As it crests near us, we swim a few strokes, extend our arms and begin our journey to shore.*

---

* For those who have not body-surfed before, here are some body-surfer basics: Stand chest high in the water with one foot in front of the other. As a wave approaches, turn your back to it and push yourself off the ocean floor, kick your feet, and start swimming fast. When the wave lifts you, thrust your arms out in front and keep them in line with your head (think of Superman or Superwoman soaring through the skies). Important caveat: you should be fit and a good swimmer. For fuller instructions, see the Grom Life at thegromlife.com/surfing/how-to-bodysurf-a-guide-to-bodysurfing and Surfer Today at surfertoday.com/surfing/how-to-bodysurf.

If the wave changes course along the way, we instinctively make adjustments to remain in alignment with its flow.

If a large wave's awesome power alarms us, or if we encounter strong turbulence during our ride, we trust that we will find ways to protect ourselves—as we always have—such as wrapping our arms and hands around our head if forcefully thrown about or diving beneath or jumping over the wave.

Much of the time, however, the ride is smooth and enjoyable and at times exhilarating—and the tumbles not as severe.

Notably, as we will see, the practices and mindsets that enhance body-surfing also enhance navigating our life currents: acceptance, trust, humility, truth, intuition, self-care, and surrender among them. And the ones that obstruct it—particularly control—also obstruct our life currents.

Another way to get a sense of the Wave is to think back to when you were a child. Probably the best Wave riders are young children. To them, life is more instinctive, at times almost an unconscious process, not so encumbered by ego, judgment, social concerns, embarrassment, shame, and external events.

Most children are thus freer to play and be in the moment, lighthearted and frivolous, yet also able to express strong emotions such as pain, fear, anger, hurt, and sadness. Consequently, riding the Wave is easier for them.

However, as we get older, we have greater responsibilities, pressures, and burdens that invoke more fear, worry, anxiety, and resentment. These demons, together with the consequent loss of self-trust, confidence, creativity, and spontaneity, erode our childlike nature.

We are thus easily removed from the present moment and reluctant—or unable—to trust our good instincts and intuition. Instead, we are driven to try to control events (and people) rather than accept and adapt to them and allow them to take their natural courses.

Thus, in a very real way, the Wave is there when we don't get in our own way. For me, my journey of staying out of my way began with the awareness of how much and in which ways my need to control obstructed my life currents.

INQUIRIES AND REFLECTIONS

- Do you ever sense a natural rhythm or flow in your daily endeavors?

- In what areas of your life is it most present?

- In dealing with uncertain or challenging situations, consider thinking or saying, "Go with the Wave," and see if it puts you more at ease.

- As an exercise, go outside in the early morning, and immerse yourself in nature. Observe the movements of the trees, clouds, and the awakening sky; feel the breeze or wind on your face; listen to the sounds of the birds; and inhale the cool freshness of the new day. As you do, note the natural unity, cohesiveness, mystery, and innate peacefulness that is all about you, and place yourself in its stream of truth, power, and wisdom. Let it flow into your life.

CHAPTER TWO

The Great Obstructor: Control

You can't stop the waves, but you can learn to surf.

—Jon Kabat-Zinn

FOLLOWING MY FACIAL SURGERIES mentioned in the introduction, I was able to settle the all-consuming lawsuit with my former business partner. I was rewarded financially but defeated—and depleted—internally. I took time off to make some sense of what I had gone through the prior five years.

As part of my healing process, I began examining the unhealthy mindsets and attitudes that had pervaded my life for so long—among them, my strong judgments, unrealistic expectations, limited thinking, know-it-all-ness, and unabated fears and worries—and had brought me to that barren place. I knew I had to change and moderate them if I was to heal.

As I reflected and wrote on these and other short-comings, one thing soon became clear to me: my need to constantly control was the cause of most of my suffering and had deprived me of any semblance of serenity—and would continue to unless I found ways to decontrol my life.

For most of my adult life, I was a major controller. I believed that the best way to satisfy my needs and achieve what I wanted in life was to control everything and everyone. Consequently, I constantly tried to change others. In my infinite wisdom, I believed I knew what was best for people, especially those closest to me, and didn't hesitate to let them know. Most of the time, I even believed I was acting benevolently.

On the outside, you could say I was successful. I graduated with high honors from a top law school, later developed and taught college-level real estate courses, and in my thirties wrote a best-selling book on real estate investing. I also owned a real estate investment company with well-known celebrities and the wealthy as clients.

However, deep in my core, I didn't feel successful or content. How could I? I was constantly enmeshed in worries, anxieties, and deep fears. Such is the fate of most controllers.

The truth is that so much of life is beyond our power to control or change. When you try to control life, the result is much the same as if you tried to grab on to a rapidly moving conveyor belt. You may slow it down temporarily, but you would ultimately get burned or dragged along.

The undeniable truth is that my controlling ways impacted all areas of my life, particularly my close relationships. Control frayed my relationship with my young son, who upon reaching adolescence, having tired of being told what was best for him all the time, became very dismissive of me. It pushed away my best friend of thirty years, who didn't speak to me for two years because

I constantly nagged him about not returning my phone calls and how he should run his business. It led to my first wife not listening to me. At first, I attributed it to her poor hearing and insisted that she take a hearing test. The doctor told us that her hearing was fine; she was just tired of listening to my constant advice.

It created tension at work from my hovering over others, constantly nitpicking, and nixing open and constructive dialogue. It also suppressed my creativity because of my constant judging, second-guessing, and apprehension about making mistakes.

The short of it was that my control-based life was consumed with *what-ifs* and *what-might-happens,* trying to attain my perceived needs and wants and not being aware of my true ones. It is no accident that I had deeper frown lines than laugh lines.

Control hinders the free and open flow of ideas, choices, and opportunities that can vastly improve our lives. It is the foremost obstructor to navigating our life currents.

In the simplest of terms, *a control-driven life is a serenity-deprived life.*

As mentioned earlier, it wasn't until I reached the brink of physical, mental, and financial exhaustion and bankruptcy that I was able to surrender the reins, lest I risk drowning in the deep sea.

I became fully aware of how much control had been restricting my life currents and how powerless I was over so many aspects in my life. I saw that control was mainly an illusion and that to the extent we could ever *gain* any semblance of control in our lives, we have to first be willing to *lose* it (let it go). Control may serve as a survival skill at times in our early years but is an obstruction to wanting more than to just survive.

I thus committed to learning ways to release my control shackles and later shared about them in *Losing Control, Finding Serenity*. As I progressed, a major gift of letting go of control became more and more apparent to me: it freed my life currents.

INQUIRIES AND REFLECTIONS

- Do you believe there is a nexus between control and serenity?
- Can you see how control limits your options and opportunities?
- Do you feel you know what's best for those closest to you? Do you let them know? How often do they do those things?
- Has a close relationship ever soured because you were too controlling?

CHAPTER THREE

Freeing the Currents

Flow with whatever is happening and let your
mind be free. Stay centered by accepting whatever
you are doing. This is the ultimate.

—Chuang Tzu

WHEN BODY-SURFERS DON'T TRY to control their rides,
they are freer to adjust and adapt to the multitude of
ways that waves can break, resulting in better, safer rides.
Similarly, when we let go of control, our life currents are
freed, creating opportunities that can vastly improve our
lives.

The dynamic is akin to removing a barrier of rocks
or tree limbs in a stream that restricts the flow of water,
causing it to pool. The currents begin to flow more freely
in diverse, unplanned routes as they move downstream—
sometimes twisting, other times splitting off in new
paths, sometimes slowing or stopping as they reach new
barriers, but all the time moving naturally.

Without removing the barrier, none of these diverse
paths—and potential opportunities—would arise. A
control-based life is like a dammed stream.

When we control, we can't flow. We thus must lose
control to find flow.

Certainly, this is much easier said than done. Control is a deeply ingrained part of the human condition. From an early age, we are all raised and taught through control. Parents, teachers, bosses, coaches—much of what they do involves controlling people and things. Control is deeply embedded in our social, economic, political, and familial fabrics.

On the home front, we control our partners and family by criticizing their choices and telling them what they should do. We control our friends by trying to change the way they are. We even control in love by lavishing gifts and doling out kind words to court pleasure, crying to churn a lover's heart, and calculating how and when to bring sexual pleasure to our mate.

Our workplaces are hotbeds for control as the concept of "survival of the fittest" is often played out through deception, intimidation, manipulation, and the drive to get ahead at all costs.

Some religions are controlling when they tell us what and how we should believe or act, lest dire consequences come our way. The political arena is rife with control practices. Misinformation about candidates and issues is broadly disseminated to discredit them and change voters' minds.

The ways we control are diverse. When we press our views or wheedle or pout to get favored treatment, we are controlling. When we judge, raise our voices (and eyebrows), or sneer, we are controlling. When we shame or guilt trip others, we are controlling. When we shove to get a better place in line or don't allow another car to enter our lane, we are controlling.

Control is often subtle and seemingly passive. Suggesting or reminding too frequently, encouraging too strongly, or preaching too intently are common control devices, as are prodding, cajoling, withdrawing from a loved one, or playing the victim or martyr.

Regardless of the reasons, to navigate our life currents in any meaningful way, we must lose control or at the very least moderate it considerably. This task is a formidable challenge. Like I did, most controllers believe that directing people and things is the best (and maybe only) way to get what they want (or think they want). When all we have known and felt comfortable and secure with is control, we are bound to feel insecure without it, especially when dealing with matters important to us.

Like changing most deeply ingrained ways, it requires a lot of practice to change our control muscle memory. I found it easier to relinquish control in small, incremental steps over time or when the stakes weren't high. As I experienced the resulting benefits, I gained more trust and confidence—and the willingness—to let go of control in more important matters.

An awareness of how much we control is an essential first step. Many of us have little inkling about how often and which ways we try to control people and things and how it harms us and those we care about.

We can see it in others but not in ourselves. We feel it when control is imposed on us but not when we impose it on others. Some will deny they control, so deeply ingrained are their control patterns. Others are steadfast (as I was) in their beliefs that their good intentions justify their constant efforts to help others see the light.

For me, the awareness came from an honest inventory of my control patterns. I had to rein in my ego, probe deeply, and ask the hard questions to see my life as it really is and myself as I truly am—blemishes and all.

This extremely uncomfortable, unsettling, and humbling process took many months, but I believe it was a necessary and beneficial one. I had to avoid easy rationalizations and self-justifications, such as I was only trying to help or look out for people or make their lives better. It remains an ongoing practice for me.

I examined whether I was too pushy, pressed too much, made repeated suggestions, offered my advice and opinions when not asked; or was too judgmental and expected too much of others; or was too impatient, intolerant, or smug. (Yes to all!) These traits were invariably intertwined with my controlling behavior and impeded aligning with the flow.

With my children, I took note of my propensity to do too much for them, try to solve their problems, or rescue them. I realized that if I continually shielded them from life's challenges, it would deprive them of the wisdom, experience, and resiliency gained from having to resolve their own struggles. (I address this subject more in chapter 19.)

With my wife, I became more aware of how often I questioned her ways of doing things, tried to influence her choices and decisions, and pressed her to do what she didn't want to do or wasn't ready to do. (I address this subject more in chapter 18.)

I also gleaned insights into my controlling ways by noting how others responded to me. When I pressured my children to do things they didn't want to do, I was often met with resistance and at times dismissiveness. When I offered unsolicited advice to friends, I was sometimes met with uncomfortable silences or diversions to other subjects.

As my controlling ways and patterns became clearer, the awareness alone significantly lessened my need to control. I continued to loosen the reins through daily decontrol affirmations, such as the following:

Today I will

- Not resist or persist.

- Not try to change others.

- Be more accepting of people and circumstances.

- Moderate my expectations of others.

- Be less judgmental.

- Honor people's choices.

- Be mindful that my way may not work for others.

As I progressed, it became clear that there was a direct correlation between letting go of control and enjoying stronger and more intimate bonds with family and friends and having less stress and anxiety and greater peace of mind and better health.

Although losing control was instrumental in freeing my life currents, I continued to have difficulty aligning with them much of the time. In writing *Losing Control, Finding Serenity*, I uncovered the main reason why: too often, I was not accepting the currents (people and things) as they are. As we will see in the next chapter, acceptance is the great aligner.

INQUIRIES AND REFLECTIONS

- Do you consider yourself a controller? Have others ever said you are controlling?

- Do you allow your loved ones to make personal choices and decisions without offering your opinion or advice?

- Are you able to sit with uncertainty or ambiguity and just let situations play out by themselves? For how long?

- As an exercise, if you feel the need to opine, advise, or change other people, instead say to yourself, "I accept them as they are."

CHAPTER FOUR

Accepting the Currents

> Let the world be as it is and learn to rock with the waves.
>
> —Joseph Campbell

IN BODY-SURFING, ONE FACT soon becomes apparent: the waves are in charge, not us. We are powerless over how they break, twist, and shift. The best way to ride them is to accept (and adjust to) them as they are.

We are similarly powerless over the many twists and turns in our lives. Whether good or bad or somewhere in between, we can better navigate our life currents when we accept them as they are.

The simple truth is that to go with the flow, you have to *accept* the flow—whether you view it as good, bad, or so-so.

Letting go of control releases or frees our life currents and provides us with the opportunity to align and flow with them, and acceptance maximizes that opportunity. As such, acceptance is the great aligner in making reality-based decisions that serve us best.

As I shared in *The Gifts of Acceptance*, through practicing acceptance, I am blessed to have established closer and more intimate bonds with friends, family, and loved ones. When others feel that we accept them as they are, they don't feel judged or less than. Trust and intimacy develop, and they feel safer in opening up to us.

The major improvement in my contentious relationship with my father in his later years is a testament to the healing power of acceptance. My dad, Morry, was only twenty-two years old when he captained thirty-five missions in the dangerous South Pacific during World War II, piloting the notoriously heavy, unsafe B-24 bomber that was prominently featured in the movie *Unbroken*.

He returned from the war a small-town hero in his native Redlands, California, having been awarded the Distinguished Flying Cross with one oak leaf cluster and the Air Medal with three oak leaf clusters.

He also returned a strict disciplinarian and an ill-prepared father to his three-year-old son—me. Growing up our relationship was never easy. Whatever I accomplished in school or sports never seemed good enough for him. When I received Bs, I was greeted with "Why didn't you get As?" When I got a hit in a Little League baseball game, he wanted to know why I didn't get two or three.

As I began to spread my wings as a teenager, our waves constantly clashed, and his punishment of choice was giving me the silent treatment—sometimes not speaking to me for months at a time. I questioned whether he loved me because I never heard him tell me that he did. My mother always assured me that my father loved me and explained to me that he just had difficulty expressing his feelings. But that never convinced me.

That all changed dramatically when I chose to accept my father as he was—flaws and all. I was able to see that he did the best he could as a very young father with limited parenting skills who didn't have the opportunities and resources (particularly educational) that he generously afforded me. I was grateful for the values he passed on to me: a strong work ethic and the ability to conduct one's affairs in a principled and ethical manner. I also realized that his not acknowledging me as I would have liked ultimately pushed me to strive harder and achieve greater success in school and my career.

I also witnessed the constant love and dedication he showed in taking care of my mother (they were married seventy-seven years!) after she suffered a debilitating stroke. And, importantly, I realized that he never meant me any harm; on the contrary, he truly wanted what was best for me.

Through my accepting my father as he was, our bond grew stronger each year, and we shared many intimate moments. In the process, I discovered that the gifts of acceptance were reciprocal. In his final years, I began hearing, "Danny, I love you."

Acceptance has also insulated me to a large extent from people who intimidate, act like control freaks, manipulate, and are just plain mean-spirited. As we will see later, when we accept such combative people as they are, their actions and words cause us considerably less stress and anxiety. It allows us to detach from their actions and not take things too personally.

Importantly, practicing acceptance helps remove our control blinders, enabling us to recognize choices and opportunities that were invisible to us before. Hence, when we accept *what is*, we are free to discover *what might be*.

By accepting the things over which we are powerless, we are no longer bound by them. There is a critical shift in focus from what we can't control or change to what we can do to make things better for ourselves or improve the situation. Acceptance empowers us by giving us this freedom. It can transport us from despair to hope and joy.

Still, it's one thing to understand the benefits of practicing acceptance. It's quite another to do it. It remains a constant challenge for me—and may be for you too—particularly in dealing with annoying or mean-spirited people.

Indeed, among other things, you may wonder why you should accept situations like these:

- Your older brother's condescending attitude
- Your father's belittling you all the time
- Your boss's nitpicking ways
- Your opponent's cheating
- Your coworker's snide remarks

If pressed to at least make an effort to accept such people as they are, you might respond with something like this:

- "Why should I have to put up with them?"
- "What good will it do me?"
- "I refuse to sacrifice my principles and values."

These concerns are valid. I've felt them many times myself—and still do, though not nearly as much or as often. It helps to understand what true acceptance means and doesn't mean in terms of navigating our life currents with less conflict and dissension.

It does not mean, for example, that we are excusing or condoning another's poor behavior. We are not. Nor does it require that we relinquish our needs or subordinate our interests and desires to those of others. It doesn't. If we feel unfairly treated or imposed upon, we can disengage, detach or, when necessary, stand our ground.

More to the point, acceptance means accepting people and things as they are *without* (or with as little as possible) judging, condemning, demeaning, or harboring negative feelings such as anger, resentment, and the like.

As such, it is the even-keeled acknowledgment of the underlying reality—the "how is" and "what is"—of the person or situation. By accepting people or circumstances in this reality-based manner, we will be able to recognize the realistic choices aligned with the situation.

This does not mean that an undesirable situation or circumstance or unpleasant person will change or go away; it *does* mean, however, that our negative feelings and counterproductive attitudes and reactions will lessen or even leave, allowing more space for light to come into our lives.

But to be clear, if something is unacceptable to us, we need not accept it. When I interviewed people while writing *The Gifts of Acceptance*, I was often asked, "Why should I accept the unacceptable?" My short answer was "Your question answers that. If something is unacceptable to you, you shouldn't accept it."

The long answer, however, is more complex. Acceptance is a personal choice each of us needs to make. What may be unacceptable for one person may not be for another. The determination is typically based on one's core beliefs and values but also on one's resentments, perceptions—and misperceptions—and willingness to forgive.

Whatever your predisposition, I would offer that before you decide something or somebody is totally unacceptable, you should first consider what consequences might follow. When I was ten years old, my father abruptly severed ties with his brother-in-law because he felt betrayed by him in a joint business enterprise. As a result, our two families permanently separated, and I was no longer able to see my closest cousins until many years later. It impacts the closeness of our relationship to this day.

The passage of time or our own shifting viewpoint can also change what was initially unacceptable to us. Helen, who lives in Australia, shared a remarkable story about the healing power of acceptance when I was writing *The Gifts of Acceptance*. Helen's third husband, of eighteen years, came home from a short trip and announced, without explanation, that he didn't want to stay married to her. Crushed, she moved to another town. Six months later, she learned that her eldest daughter from a prior marriage left her husband and children and moved in with Helen's ex-husband.

I think most people would agree that if there ever was unacceptable behavior, this clearly qualified. Helen was very angry and resentful and had a nervous breakdown. She became estranged from her four children and led a life of bitterness and regret for twelve years, until she finally realized that the onus was on her to change her unhappy life.

Through therapy and self-help programs, she slowly found a way to live in acceptance of what had happened. In Helen's words,

"I learnt that by feeling sorry for myself and blaming everyone around me the only person that was suffering and hurting was me. I had finally accepted that what happened between my ex and my daughter happened and there was nothing anyone could do about it, and nor should we.

"Strangely because my attitude had changed and the rest of my family realized I had accepted the situation, life became so much better. I am once again looked upon as the matriarch of my family of four children, twelve grandchildren, and five great-grandchildren. I now have a great relationship with all of the family, including my daughter and son-in-law. Once I accepted that he was no longer my 'ex-husband' and was in fact my son-in-law, life was so much easier."

Helen demonstrated tremendous courage and understanding in finally accepting what had been intolerable. Yet also, her story illustrates that with time, searching reflection, and forgiveness, the unacceptable (and its impact on us) can eventually give way to acceptance, particularly as our negative feelings subside. Only when we fully process these feelings can we let go of what happened and constructively move forward with our lives.

Because acceptance facilitates navigating our life currents in so many ways, we must continually practice it. I have found acceptance-based intentions helpful. Below are some I use:

I intend to

- Be more aware of what I am powerless to change.
- Honor my loved one's personal choices.

- Not judge my friends.
- Be more understanding of people's shortcomings.
- Remember that no one is perfect.
- Not take things too personally.

Even though I am not always able to fulfill these intentions, even partial success has helped me be more accepting.

Fundamentally, acceptance is a *choice* we make. We can choose to accept people and things as they are or not. I sincerely believe that if we choose acceptance, the very act births opportunities that can transform—often dramatically—our life, the lives of others, and, I believe, the world.

We have thus far looked at the two fundamentals for riding the Wave and navigating our life currents: losing control and practicing acceptance. As I have improved in doing both over time, I have been blessed with more peace and serenity than I could ever have imagined.

However, my progress was (and is) repeatedly stymied by the impact of certain potent "wave obstructors." These obstructors have a dual effect on successfully riding the Wave: they induce us to control more and to accept less. They remain an ongoing challenge for me and, I believe, many other people as well.

Part 2 explores how we can overcome or at least reduce these obstructors. One of the most difficult ones for me to overcome is solely of my own doing: my propensity to judge people and things.

INQUIRIES AND REFLECTIONS

- What things are unacceptable to you? Have any changed with time?

- Does your acceptance threshold vary depending on your relationship with the person? Are you more or less accepting with your family and loved ones?

- Do you recognize when you are powerless over changing someone or something? What are the indications?

- Have you noticed that as you have become more accepting, you have become less controlling?

PART TWO

Wave Obstructors

CHAPTER FIVE

Judging Other Riders

When you judge another, you do not define them,
you define yourself.

—Wayne Dyer

WHEN BODY-SURFERS JUDGE OR criticize how other surf-
ers ride their waves—the choices they are making or
what they are doing wrong or shouldn't be doing—they
are distracted from riding their own waves well.

Similarly, when we judge or criticize the choices and
actions of others, our focus is on finding flaws with them.
That diverts our attention (and intention) from where
it can do us the most good: ourselves and how we can
improve our lives.

In terms of the Wave, when we are focused on how
others navigate their life currents, we can't navigate our
own well.

Because I am a controller by nature, judging has
been such an ingrained habit that, much of the time, I am
not aware that I'm doing it. One reason is that judging
takes many forms. Some are overt; others are subtle.
Criticizing, admonishing, shaming, and being smug,
dismissive, or sarcastic are prevalent ways we judge. Snide
smiles and sneers and other forms of body language also

convey judgment. Judging at its worst breeds intolerance. Unfortunately, I've done them all.

I am not proposing that we shouldn't express our views and beliefs about matters that are important to us. I believe we should. And I am also not suggesting that we shouldn't discern or assess and judge whether certain behavior or actions by others may not be good for us or cause us harm. These kinds of preventive and protective assessments are wise and prudent.

Hence, if a person is driving recklessly, yelling profanities, or acting belligerently, it is certainly proper to judge whether his or her actions are harmful or disrespectful toward us and respond appropriately.

I'm alluding to the gratuitous, self-righteous type of judgments that don't directly impact us, or, as some might say, "It's none of our business." These include judgments like "You're doing it all wrong," "He talks too much," or "They're way too indulgent with their kids" or critiques like "What a poor color choice for their home," "Their yard is unkempt," or "She's always so negative."

These kinds of know-it-all-ness are prevalent in most of my judgments—that I know better than another. Yet little do I know or consider the reasons or contexts in which people act or make choices. And rarely do I account for my personal biases and prejudices.

Not surprising, many of my judgments have proved to be dead wrong. During my first year of law school, I harshly judged one of my classmates while waiting for the instructor to arrive. The classroom had rows of desks tiered upward toward the back on rising planes. My classmate suddenly jumped on top of his desk in the rear and boldly walked (and put his dirty shoes) on top of other classmates' desks to the front of the room.

Everyone laughed except me. I was very angry. I thought, "What a jerk and a-hole. All he wants is attention." I didn't want to have anything to do with him after that.

Fast-forward five years after we graduated law school. This "jerk" became my most trusted friend and confidant and later was the best man at my wedding!

He did continue to draw a lot of attention, though. He selflessly served as the public defender of Los Angeles County for over fifteen years, supervising over seven hundred attorneys, and was widely recognized for his efforts in helping reform state and national criminal justice systems.

So I guess I misjudged! And the further irony of it is not lost on me: his last name was Judge. I miss Mike dearly.

The thing is, if I am not mindful, I am still prone to judging harshly. More recently, I again wrongfully judged a longtime friend for not responding to an email I sent him inviting him to the premier of my wife's one-woman show, *Tragic Magic—A Story of Recovery*, which was about her journey of repair, recovery, and hope from severe trauma and addiction.

As my resentment was beginning to build, I received an email from my friend letting me know that he had been in Mexico for his son's wedding and that the email address I had used was for a company he no longer worked for. And he said yes, he definitely wanted to see my wife's show!

When you think about it, who wants to be judged? I certainly don't, and I'm pretty sure most people don't either. I become resentful—and I'm not going to confide in that person. I then ask myself, Why do I continue to judge so much? What is my motive? What purpose does it serve? Does it make me feel better or superior in some way? Maybe it does for a short moment, but it's a sure sign of my lack of humility. Do I think it will change or help the other person in some way? Sometimes I do, but it rarely does, if at all. And no one's ever thanked me for my judgments, that's for sure.

It has also occurred to me that my judging may be an indication of some shortcoming in myself. Concerning the incident with my law school classmate, for example, I was a reserved and even shy person. Perhaps seeing someone be so bold, carefree, and out there accentuated my own flaw. And with my other friend, it was indicative of my tendency to speculate negatively about things.

A friend once shared with me that her judging is usually a mechanism for not having to look at herself. To counter that, when she finds herself judging others harshly, she asks, "What's going on with me?"

I've also noticed that I am more judgmental when I'm stressed or frustrated. During the unnerving early days of the COVID-19 pandemic, I had little patience and was easily agitated over little things. Judging became a convenient way of venting and avoiding dealing with my core feelings, particularly fear and anxiety.

On one occasion, I reacted strongly when a close relative asked me to share a video with my friends concerning a disgruntled scientist who was making disparaging remarks about a well-known scientist who was playing a prominent public role in helping combat the pandemic. After viewing the vitriolic video, I had serious doubts about its veracity and accusations. My research found evidence that disputed the disgruntled scientist's claims, including having once been fired by the accused scientist.

I admonished my relative for promoting the video to others without first fact-checking the assertions. I forwarded him the research that I had uncovered. But that didn't deter him. He was convinced about the merits of the scientist's claim and was adamant about what he was doing.

The truth of the matter is that I judged my relative harshly for his beliefs and actions. I felt the video was untruthful and wanted him to stop—signs of a true controller and judger. We should instead be cognizant that what we say or do *does* matter.

In a very real way, I believe judging is a diversionary tactic that distracts us from taking stock of ourselves and improving our own shortcomings. It doesn't change what people believe or how they act in any meaningful sense. If anything, judging puts people on the defensive, and their views become hardened. There is a greater chance that people will consider contrarian views when they are presented in a thoughtful, respectful manner.

I have come to believe judging may be such an ingrained part of the human condition—likely from as early as our formative years—that it can never be totally abated, short of our becoming saints. However, it can be significantly lessened with awareness, willingness, and, above all, acceptance.

Harshly judging ourselves also impacts our going with the flow. We should be mindful of the inner critic who is constantly judging us and telling us we're doing things wrong, we're not good or nice enough, or we don't have what it takes. This internal voice also creates doubt and the myriad of other mistruths. Take a minute—just one—and listen to it, and you will readily see what I mean.[1] Being compassionate and accepting of ourselves does a lot to silence its chatter, as does being aware that almost everything it says is untrue or unimportant and mainly a byproduct of our fears and insecurities.

When we accept people and things as they are, we have little need to judge them. Like me, my relative had the right to express his views and make his own choices during the pandemic—provided they didn't harm me or those I care about. I could have just accepted that, politely declined his request, and let it go instead of getting all worked up over it.

Kahlil Gibran in *Sand and Foam* offers some good reasons for and benefits of not disparaging the views of others: "I have learned silence from the talkative, toleration from the intolerant, and kindness from the unkind; yet strange, I am ungrateful to these teachers."[2]

The short of it is that I see no benefit in disparaging the views and choices of others. It only impedes the flow. Therefore, I continue to ask, "What purpose does it serve?" I haven't found a good answer yet.

Let's next look at an obstructor that is a close companion of judging and invariably stirs the waters of disappointment and resentment: high expectations.

INQUIRIES AND REFLECTIONS

- In which ways do you judge others?
- What mindsets are behind your judgments? Do they serve a useful purpose?
- How often do you judge yourself? Are those judgments about the same kinds of things that you judge others for?
- As a revealing exercise, make note of your judgments for a day—or even half a day. Be sure to include the silent ones you say to yourself.

CHAPTER SIX

Expectant Waters

When one's expectations are reduced to zero, one
really appreciates everything one does have.

—Stephen Hawkins

WHEN BODY-SURFERS HEAD TO the beach with high
expectations that the waves will be great, and they aren't,
they are disappointed. And when they expect or rely on
waves breaking in certain ways, and they don't, they are
ill-prepared to make the adjustments necessary to avoid
potential tumbles.

Similarly, when we expect others to act—or not act—
in certain ways, and they don't, or when we rely on certain
outcomes, and they don't come to pass, we are disappointed
and ill-prepared to make the adjustments that would allow
us to align with what is actually occurring.

We all have expectations. They are a natural part of
wanting a better and more content life. Thus, we expect
our family and friends to act kindly and responsibly
toward us, for our work to provide us with certain
financial benefits and security, for our children to be
truthful and diligent in their studies, for teachers to be
trained and able, for our leaders to govern honestly, and
so on.

Unrealistic or unreasonably high expectations obstruct the natural flow. Whether assertive or subtle, our
expecting too much of others pressures them to act and
be other than they aspire to. It easily becomes a double-
edged sword; we are resentful that they don't meet our
expectations, and they resent our not accepting them as
they are.

High expectations also lead to disappointments. The
grander the expectation, the grander the disappointment.
Not long ago, I had high expectations that addiction
recovery centers would gladly welcome the opportunity
for their members to attend my wife's one-woman show,
Tragic Magic—A Story of Recovery, at a discounted ticket
price of only five dollars. I spent the better part of two
days contacting numerous recovery centers to let them
know about the show and the special pricing. Not one
center took up the offer. I was more than disappointed. I
was disheartened.

I had another big disappointment when trying to sell
my beautiful older convertible that I infrequently drove
and was costing me a lot of money to insure and maintain. I learned about a local car event held twice a month
on Sunday mornings in Malibu that was attended by
hundreds of car enthusiasts. I spent Saturday afternoon
washing and detailing the car in anticipation of strong
buyer interest. I drove to the event early Sunday morning, anticipating that I would find a buyer. Upon arriving,
however, not one car was there. Unbeknownst to me, the
event had been cancelled for the remainder of the year.

When I later moderated my expectations about
selling the car, something unforeseen happened. My wife

drove it when her car was in the shop, and she enjoyed the car so much, it has become a fun weekend car for the two of us.

This incident once again confirmed to me that life's ebb and flow pays no heed to our expectations. While being hopeful and even optimistic about outcomes is fine, it behooves us not to be overly expectant or reliant on things occurring the way we want or expect them to—or at least be prepared if they don't.

Many Eastern philosophies teach that our suffering stems from the difference or space between what we want or expect things to be and the way they really are. I have found that to be true in so many areas of my life.

In my painting endeavors, for example, it seems that whenever I form high expectations following a good start to a painting, my creativity stops flowing intuitively, and the work is impacted.

On the home front, when my loved ones don't follow my recommendations or advice, I sometimes feel dismissed. And at work, when business associates don't meet my expectations, I am perturbed.

Expecting too much of ourselves also impacts the flow. While it's important to try our best, set goals, and hold ourselves accountable, when we expect too much of ourselves, we can easily find ourselves forcing, pressing, and thus putting ourselves out of alignment with the natural flow of events.

Numerous times on the tennis court, I have played against opponents who constantly berate themselves for making errors, only to make more. And when I set high expectations for a match, I find myself pressing to meet them, and my play suffers.

One type of expectation that is particularly detrimental in relationships is the unexpressed kind where we expect others to know what we want or how we are feeling. I felt the brunt of these mind-reading expectations early on. My father always expected my sister and me to know when we hurt his feelings by something we may have said or done. But he wouldn't say what it was, and we usually had no clue. Instead, he would give us the silent treatment, sometimes for days, until we probed or guessed what our misdeed was and then apologized for it.

I feel it's important to let people know if we are upset at something they said or did, rather than remain silent, as it will fester and come out stronger later. Other people's actions may not have been intentional, or they may have been unaware of how much they impacted us, or we may simply have misconstrued something they said. Whatever may be the case, thoughtfully conveying our feelings provides an opportunity to discuss and hopefully resolve what has transpired.

The key is to find the appropriate balance between what we can or should reasonably and realistically expect of others or things (or ourselves) and considering whether our expectations are too high or unreasonable.

In moderating my expectations, I try to examine what underlies them. Am I looking for someone to fulfill certain needs or wants—maybe the need to be heard by my children or a close friend, be nurtured by my wife, or be acknowledged by my peers? If so, I am likely being overly expectant.

Others can be supportive and caring, but most often, our needs are something that only we can fulfill; our happiness and contentment depend mainly on us, not others. High expectations place the focus too much on others, and we lose sight of what we can do for ourselves.

The Al-Anon twelve-step program aptly expresses this notion with the slogan "Let it begin with me." An important corollary is that the more we look to ourselves to satisfy our wants and needs, the less we need look to others.

I also consider whether my expectations are aimed at trying to change another's ways that bother me or actually trying to help them. But the simple truth is that people will change when and if *they* choose or are able to do so, not when I want them to. And more often, I don't even know what's best for me, let alone others.

I have learned that most of the time my expectations are not that important in the overall scheme of things. They may seem important to me at the time but not after I take a moment to reflect upon them. Some underlying concern or fear often impels me to believe that more is at stake than what truly is.

I have found that when I expect less, I accept more, control less, and align better with my life currents.

One specific obstructor has always impacted my riding the Wave expansively: limited thinking.

INQUIRIES AND REFLECTIONS

- How often are your expectations aimed at trying to change others? Do they change?
- Are your expectations of family and loved ones higher than they are for others? Why?
- How do you feel when others expect too much from you?
- Do you expect more from others or yourself?

CHAPTER SEVEN

Limiting the Currents

If you accept a limiting belief, then it will become
a truth for you.

—Louise Hay

WHEN WE ARE RELUCTANT to body-surf different kinds of
waves at new beaches, we limit opportunities for discovery,
improvement, and pleasure. In much the same manner,
limited or negative thinking restricts our life currents,
resulting in lost opportunities and enriching experiences.

Limited thinking is an obstructor that takes comfort
in maintaining the status quo. I gained insight as to how
my limited thinking short-circuits opportunities during
a fly-fishing trip with my son to the Sian Ka'an Biosphere,
a government-protected nature and wildlife reserve at the
southern tip of Mexico. The guided expedition, called
"Fly-fishing for the Mind," was led by two therapists,
who taught us how our life issues—frustration, disappointment, control, impatience, and the like—also
arise when fly-fishing.

My son thinks expansively about life's possibilities—
particularly those involving fun and adventure. His
typical mindset is "Let's do it" and "It will be a lot of fun."
Unlike him, I tend to think restrictively, such as "That's

not a good idea," or "That's not what's been planned," or "That won't work."

Had I adhered to my ways during our trip, I would have missed out on some highly rewarding experiences. On the second day of the trip, twelve of us in three small motorboats took a half-day tour. We were entertained by sea turtles and dolphins during the first part of the excursion. Snorkeling at the second largest barrier reef in the world was scheduled for the second part.

While motoring to the barrier reef, we approached a primitive wood bridge that led to a small fishing village where our guides lived. My son asked our guide if the village fishermen caught lobster. When the guide nodded yes, my son enthusiastically proposed, "Let's go to the village and buy some lobsters and take them back to the lodge for dinner tonight."

The first words out of my mouth were "If we do that, we won't be able to go snorkeling at the barrier reef."

"Why?" my son quipped.

Before I could respond, the others in the boats chimed in, saying they also wanted to visit the village and buy lobsters. What followed was a delightful visit to Punta Allen, a small unspoiled Caribbean paradise, in which we engaged the locals and experienced their simple lifestyle.

Despite my concerns, our guides gladly extended our tour so we could still go snorkeling at the barrier reef. And to top things off, the lodge's cook prepared a sumptuous lobster feast for everyone, and my son was saluted for taking the initiative.

Near the end of our trip, my son asked if we could stay a night in Cancún so we could be together with our travel mates and enjoy a beautiful Caribbean beachfront resort before returning home. My first thoughts once again were limiting: we would have to pay to change flights and end our stay in a bustling resort area after spending a week in splendid tranquility. Fortunately, I caught my "can't do" thinking and told him, "If you can make the arrangements, let's do it!"

The white-sand beach and majestic turquoise waters of Cancún were great, but nothing in the trip compared to the special ritual we were blessed to experience with the members of our fly-fishing troupe. We had a torch-lit gathering at a secluded bay adjacent to our hotel where we formed a circle under a palapa. One of the leaders faced me and offered a special gift by sharing what he liked and appreciated about me. I then did the same in return. Each person then turned to another and exchanged like gifts.

It was one of the most enriching experiences I have ever had—one that would never have happened had I remained mired in my limited thinking. By the end of the trip, it had become clearer to me that when I limit my thinking, I limit my life currents. I deprive myself of opportunities to explore, discover, and enjoy.

Like most people, I have regrets about missed opportunities—things I wished I would have done or things I missed out on. My limited thinking was largely responsible for such "shouldas, wouldas, couldas."

One time in particular my negative thinking and speculations caused me to miss out on an exciting opportunity was when I turned down an invitation by a skilled Mexican fisherman—whom I had befriended while on vacation—to join him on his boat in an annual fishing derby in San Blas, Mexico. The year before, he had won a new car in a major fishing derby in Acapulco.

At first, my heart jumped. It was a once-in-a-lifetime opportunity to learn from a masterful fisherman. But in no time, my negative thinking flooded my mind:

"I won't feel comfortable sleeping in a small boat."

"I will feel out of place being around Mexican fishermen and not speaking fluent Spanish."

"I would have to be away from the office for over a week."

"I am totally inexperienced in big-game fishing."

I have regretted not going ever since.

Limited thinking can also deprive us of valuable learning opportunities—a lesson I learned while playing tennis with less-skilled players, particularly those with unorthodox styles. My typical thoughts were "Playing with him will mess up my game" or "It will be no fun." Not surprisingly, it invariably did mess up my game, and I didn't have any fun!

I now realize that such thinking squelches opportunities to improve my game. As a senior's tournament player, I need to know how to adjust my game and strategy to play against all types of players—including those with unconventional games. The best way to do that is to practice with *all* types of players.

Currently when playing against such players, I view it as an opportunity to improve other aspects of my game, such as drop shots, lobs, and overheads. More importantly, I have fun.

In reflecting on why I am so adept at coming up with reasons *not* to do things instead of reasons to *do* them, I have discovered two main reasons: The first is my not wanting to leave or stretch outside my comfort zone. Underlying that is the fear of change and uncertainty.

The other is my not being aware or mindful enough of my restrictive thinking. And so I gain awareness when I simply ask, "Is my thinking limited or negative in some way?"

Most often, the answer is yes. A recent example was when my wife and I decided to add a patio trellis to our small vacation home. I was set on it being made of durable redwood. While driving by a nearby home, my wife noticed workers installing a white vinyl trellis over the home's front porch. She remarked that we should consider doing the same because it would be less expensive and require far less maintenance.

True to form, I promptly dismissed her suggestion. I wanted solid wood, not flimsy vinyl. A few minutes later, I caught myself being too insistent and thought to ask the big question: "Is my thinking limited again?" Realizing it was, I told my wife that I was open to considering vinyl. She ordered samples of the product, and it turned out that the vinyl was strong because it was layered over an aluminum base.

My "stinking thinking" occurred again when we were in New York for her performance of *Tragic Magic* at the United Solo festival, the nation's largest solo-performance festival. My wife needed to find small cushions to attach to the leg bottoms of the chair that served as a prop for her show to avoid a screeching noise caused by moving the chair to different places on the stage during her performance.

As we were walking in search of pads, my wife noticed the store sign "MJ Trimmings—Est. 1937" on the opposite side of heavily trafficked Sixth Avenue and wanted to see if they had cushions. I immediately dismissed the idea, saying, "They won't have cushions there. The window sign says trimmings and decorations."

Not persuaded, she insisted on visiting the store. Inside the store, just as I thought, the store had a wide assortment of trimmings, buttons, and decorative items. Still undeterred, my wife explained her needs to a salesperson, who guided her to an obscure part of the store where she found small velcro pads perfectly suited for the chair.

Knowing my propensities, I now try to wait a few beats to discard the immediate "This won't work" and "We shouldn't do" reactions. Such first-thought negations prevent me from giving due consideration to other choices. They are the language of the inner critic that constantly tells me "It's a bad idea" or "It won't work," along with the myriad other mistruths it chatters.

In their place, when considering something new or different I now ponder, "*What would it feel or be like?*"

Most often, the situation is not as I had thought or feared. In fact, taking the time to visualize how doing something new or different would be—and getting in touch with the feelings that come up for me—is quite often liberating. This practice cuts through my negativity and opens my mind to trying new currents—and many of them have led to enriching experiences, such as the one I had with my son while fly-fishing.

Limiting our life currents is bad enough. It's even worse when we are not in the water altogether. One obstructor does that extremely well: avoidance.

INQUIRIES AND REFLECTIONS

- Are you a creature of habit? How do you view change?

- What opportunities have you forgone because of your limited or negative thinking?

- How do you catch yourself from your limited thinking?

- As an exercise, try asking yourself, How would that feel? or What would that be like? when considering new things.

CHAPTER EIGHT

Avoiding the Currents

Engulfed with anger,
We retreat.
Ensnared by fear,
We hide.

Webbed by doubts,
We avoid.
Immersed in pities,
We remain
In exile—
With no default mode.

To return,
Joust the fears,
Lose the anger
Embrace your truth, and
Face the danger.

—Daniel A. Miller, "Default Mode"

IT GOES WITHOUT SAYING that we can't body-surf waves—or even swim—when we aren't in the water, whether because of the cold, fear, or just not wanting to get wet.

Similarly, we can't navigate or flow with our life currents when we avoid, deny, or withdraw from them. Instead, we dwell in a lonely alternate reality where we are prone to making poor choices.

Avoidance comes in many forms: denial, wishful thinking, procrastination, withdrawal, the turning of a blind eye, or simply the belief that things aren't as they are. It can also manifest itself as not coming to grips with a serious financial matter, a deteriorating relationship, a child's drug abuse, or a serious health issue.

Fear is behind a lot of avoidance, but not always. I often procrastinate in dealing with mundane but nonetheless important matters because they are too cumbersome, time-consuming, or boring—or I just don't feel like doing them. The unfortunate paradox is that such avoidance prevents us from recognizing the choices we have that could alleviate the very concerns or problems we are shunning.

My prolonged delay in addressing the rapidly deteriorating housing market during the Great Recession of 2008 when trying to sell our home was a costly example. My wife and I had purchased and moved into another house before selling the home, an architecturally designed home with magnificent views of the San Fernando Valley.

In the first two weeks the house was on the market, I turned down offers that were 10 to 15 percent below our asking price. Although I had read a few articles about the weakening market, my ego-based denial mindset kept wishfully whispering that it wouldn't impact the sale of our "special" home.

As prices continued to tumble in the coming months, I still resisted facing market realities. After ten months of making mortgage payments and paying property taxes for the two homes, the pain—in the form of loss of sleep, anxiety, and financial drain—lifted my denial blinders. I ended up selling the home for 25 percent less than the initial offers, leaving us with a lot of shouldas and couldas—and a lot less money.

Regrettably, this wasn't the first time that my denial proved costly. Looking back, many of my denials were based on the persistent belief that I had the power to change or make things better when in fact I didn't.

I fell prey to what I call the *superman (or superwoman) myth.* Members of this not-too-exclusive club include control freaks, perfectionists, dedicated problem solvers, and others with inflated egos and a shortage of humility, who believe they can conquer reality—or that it somehow doesn't apply to them—and persist in trying to find solutions to problems that aren't ready to be solved.

The most consequential case of my denial was avoiding facing up to how my life had become unmanageable in trying to solve my wife's escalating drinking problem.[1]

From the time we met, we had an immediate, soulful love connection between us. It was the third marriage for each of us, and we shared many of the same interests, values, and life desires. The first three years were fun, full, and exciting.

However, after getting married and having a child, my wife's drinking increased markedly, and our close bond began to deteriorate. Having been through the pain and remorse of divorce twice before, each with a child suffering the consequences, I could not bear the thought of it happening again.

I was at a loss about what to do except, as a dedicated problem solver, try my best to "solve" my wife's drinking problem. I constantly tried reasoning with her to stop drinking. I encouraged her to see a therapist. I wrote letters pleading with her to "see the light" about what was happening to our family. I even threatened to leave several times. All to no avail. If anything, it made matters worse. When several times she refrained from drinking for a week, I wishfully thought the problem was over—until her drinking resumed again.

Through it all, I felt my wife was in strong denial of her addiction. Not once did I consider that I, too, was in denial—of how out of control my own life had become because of my obsession in trying to solve a problem over which I was powerless.

At the recommendation of a therapist, I began attending Al-Anon twelve-step-program meetings for people whose friends and family have drinking problems. I did so begrudgingly for the first few months, rationalizing that it wasn't me who had the drinking problem.

In time, however, the light of awareness began to shine through as I became more aware that alcoholism was a lascivious disease over which I was powerless. I then began focusing on improving my own shortcomings—and there were many.

Two years later, my wife also overcame her denial and—on her own—sought recovery in a twelve-step program. At this writing, she is approaching twenty years of sobriety and sponsors other women in their recovery efforts.

Thanks to overcoming our denials, our love bond is now stronger than ever. I am deeply grateful for how blessed our lives are today.

Procrastination is another kind of avoidance that removes us from our life currents. When we delay addressing our problems, opportunities to resolve them pass by, and unattended problems can easily mushroom into larger and unmanageable ones that require more time, energy, and expense to resolve—if in fact they can be.

I lost almost half my nose because I kept putting off seeing a dermatologist to remove what was at the time a small cancerous lesion on it. What would have been a little inconvenience turned out to be a major life-changing one.

The undeniable truth is that when we bury troublesome matters, they don't disappear. They simply remain in the far reaches of our minds, where they are nourished and magnified.

Because procrastination is usually fear based, a worst-case scenario exercise can help remove the blinders. Sometimes when I am hesitant to address or act on something important, I try to project the worst things that could happen through a series of what-if inquiries so I get everything on the table. As I do this, I try to separate fact from fiction and then map out an action plan, should my worst fears materialize. It's been my experience most of the time they don't—at least not in the foreboding ways I had imagined. The perceived problems feel less ominous, allowing me to face the challenges head-on.

If I am uncertain where to begin, I test the waters by taking the first indicated step. It may be by responding to an upsetting email, disputing an excessive service charge, or making an uncomfortable outreach call. Whatever it may be, taking the first step lightens the burden.

Withdrawal is still another harmful form of avoidance. When our burdens and pressures overwhelm us, it's often easier to withdraw into our inner sanctum of painful thoughts and self-pity rather than to confront vital issues head-on. The problem is that when we withdraw, we leave the currents entirely.

When I was younger, my withdrawals impacted almost everything in my life. Sometimes I would withdraw from family and loved ones for days at a time when I felt slighted, mistreated, or misjudged. I am certainly not proud of that. They would feel rejected and abandoned—and rightly so.

At work, I would isolate myself and not take proper care of my business. My creative outlets of writing and painting ceased. In sports, my performance became lackluster. And in intimate relations, my sex drive waned.

Like procrastination, the danger with withdrawal is that it becomes self-perpetuating; the longer our withdrawal, the more difficult our return, and by the time we finally do, the damage may have already been done.

To prevent negative momentum, we need to nip withdrawal in the bud, lest it fester and propel us deeper into our aloneness. I have found that returning from personal exile requires me to lean into and process my core feelings and emotions—be it grief, sadness, rejection, loneliness, or the like. It's not easy. I have to mollify my ego, move into acceptance of what is real in the moment and needs my attention, and acknowledge what my part may have been in what caused me to withdraw.

In general, I have learned that my propensity toward avoidance or denial relates to two mental states: my unawareness or nonacceptance of the underlying reality of a situation and my unwillingness to address what is.

Hence, I must be aware, accepting, and willing. When I'm not, my pain and suffering due to my continuing avoidance usually boil over before I muster the courage and willingness to address what is. Had I not been in denial with the sale of my home, I could have accepted a lower price in the beginning and saved a bundle of money—and avoided a lot of sleepless nights.

I am now more aware of my avoidance mindsets. Some signs are the thoughts "Am I dismissing or downplaying something important?" "Am I looking to take the easy way out?" "Am I feeling anxious about something?" "Am I being truthful with myself?" and "Am I feeling down?" The answers to these questions usually shed light on what I may be denying or avoiding. On some level, I usually know the problems are there and just need to muster the courage to deal with them.

One obstructor not only severely hampers going with the flow but also was nearly my downfall: rage.

INQUIRIES AND REFLECTIONS

- What things might you be avoiding or denying currently?

- What things typically cause you to withdraw from others? What feelings are manifested for you? What does it take for you to return?

- How often do you put off doing something for another day (such as filing, balancing your accounts, scheduling a repair or service person, etc.) because it's a drag?

- How many times do you usually think about doing something before you actually do it? Couldn't that time be put to better use?

CHAPTER NINE

Raging Waters

Raging waters crash to shore,
Raging riders crash to core.
Raging waters restore,
Raging riders continue to roar.

—Daniel A. Miller, "Raging Riders"

BODY-SURFING WHEN ANGRY IS a fool's errand. We are
prone to miscalculation and precipitous decisions—and
certainly, there's little joy in the ride. Similarly, when we
are angry or resentful, we are out of sync with our life
currents.

Regrettably, I all too often raged when I was younger.
It made me feel powerful—especially the initial roars.
The problem was, to paraphrase the old saying, "I took
the poison and waited for the other person to die." But
they never did!

Certainly, no one can expect to lead a life totally
devoid of anger. Letting off steam is healthy. For the most
part, though, we forget about the rude driver who abruptly
cut in front of us by the time we reach our destination or
about the lengthy wait to speak with customer service
about a computer or internet glitch by the time we have
lunch.

But unbridled, deep-rooted anger and resentment are much different. They are emotional tidal waves—often arising from betrayal, abandonment, rejection, strong abuse, and the like—that cause us to become obsessed and possessed, and we are usually unable to let them go, no matter how hard we try.

I painfully learned that rage and strong resentment act like razor-sharp boomerangs; whatever force they may generate initially ricochets back multifold, severely impacting us emotionally and spiritually with shame, remorse, and often depression.

My longstanding rage and seeking of vengeance against the business partner whom I felt had betrayed me in my time of need contributed to the breakdown of my first marriage, the deterioration of the close bond with my young son, and my missing doctors' appointments for the early removal of a minor skin cancer lesion on my nose—a dereliction that required six major surgeries to eradicate the cancer, which had spread voraciously through my face, and reconstruct my nose.

On another occasion, my rageful behavior frightened the daylights out of my six-year-old daughter. During a road trip, my wife pulled the car into a gas station to fill up. We exchanged some heated words that I can't even remember now. As she was slowly driving back out onto the street, she reprimanded, "We should have left you at home!"

Absolutely furious, I immediately opened the door and hopped out of the car as it was moving, childishly shouting, "I'm going home." My wife quickly applied the brakes, bringing the car to a halt. My startled daughter, sitting in her car seat, began sobbing uncontrollably, saying, "Daddy, I'm only a little girl. I'm only a little girl."

It broke my heart to see the absolute fear and trauma I had brought upon my dear little girl. I still cringe with sadness and deep remorse for my behavior as I write these very words. Clearly, my raging had taken its toll on my family.

I am embarrassed to admit that those were not isolated events. There were others, mainly with family, usually triggered by being falsely accused or abruptly dismissed.

I knew I had to find ways to quickly quell the roars, lest my entire being would continue to be engulfed in escalading riptides and undertows. In the depths of such abysses, I was prone to being self-destructive and making serious mistakes.

An important key for me was learning to accept people and things as they are. The first thing I do upon wakening in the morning is get on my knees by the bed in prayer position and recite the Serenity Prayer.[1] I then recite it again outdoors in front of my peaceful olive tree before having breakfast.

I am thus more fully aware, from the start of my day, of the vast number of things—and people—that I cannot change and that my serenity depends on my willingness to accept them as they are.

The prayer works best for me when I apply its words to the specific situations and circumstances that I am currently facing or dealing with. It may be people who have provoked my anger, business or financial concerns, relationships that are going awry, and a myriad of other life happenings.

Starting off my days in this manner brings a calmness that deflects any emotional tsunamis that may arise—at least to the extent that I can pause and process them in a more even-keeled manner instead of immediately going bonkers.

I also try not to take peoples' disturbing words and actions so personally, recognizing that they reveal more about them (and where they're at) than me. That lessens the bothersome feeling that others are intentionally doing things to me.

I once held a grudge against a theater creative director whose productions we had financially supported for many years for his not attending my wife's one-person show during its run. We both invited him multiple times, but he didn't respond to our invitations, and I resented his hurting my wife's feelings and not being grateful for our past support.

Two obstructors parlayed my resentment. One was my assumption that he had hurt my wife's feelings. I was wrong. When I later I shared my criticisms of him with my wife, she informed me that her feelings in fact were not hurt, saying, "I just accept that's the way he is, and I don't take any of it personally." (She's a wonderful teacher!)

The other factor was my high expectations, given that I knew how involved he was with his many duties for his own theatrical productions. As I reflected, I saw that I made unconditional gifts of support into conditional ones, and that is not how I wish to give. With awareness of both these factors, I was able to let go of my lingering resentment.

Another factor in releasing anger and resentment is that, upon honest reflection, I am able to see I usually had some part in what had transpired, even if it were a small one. On the home front, for example, whenever my wife and I exchange heated words or are at an uncomfortable impasse, I know to ask myself, "Did I have any part— even a small one—in what just happened?" Invariably, the truthful, non-self-righteous answer is yes, and that defuses my anger.

I make the same inquiry in other situations. Recently I was upset at a designer who had mistakenly ordered twice as much tile as we needed for our bathroom, and it wasn't returnable. After steaming for a couple of hours, I cooled down after realizing that I was partly responsible for what had occurred; namely, I neglected to review the order before it was placed.

I'm also mindful not to repress my anger, lest it fester until it eventually erupts. To become more aware of my anger, I look for its clues. Withdrawing or closing up are usually disguised forms of anger. Snapping at people or being overly critical or judgmental of them can be as well. Feeling down or depressed can be repressed anger and resentment. Anger can also manifest itself physically in such forms as muscle tightness, sore back, and headaches.

Whatever the source, once I am aware of my anger, I try to defuse it right away. Exercise is an important outlet for me. In order to deal with the rage I had toward my former partner, I took karate classes and regularly hit a punching bag attached to my carport. That helped a lot. Physical release also frees my mind from its obsessive, negative thoughts.

At other times, I vent my anger in writing. I take a pad and start writing away, safely expressing all my nasty thoughts about the person or thing that triggered my anger—and then tear it up. Or I'll write an email and then delete it.

Still, like with Helen in chapter 4, sometimes anger and resentment can be so unrelenting, I'm unable to step out of its cesspool until I am able to *find* forgiveness. That's the only thing that fully extricated me from the shackles of my rage toward my former business partner. A wise friend one day asked whether I could ever forgive my partner. I remember my response so clearly: "Are you kidding! Look at what he's done to me. Why should I forgive him?" My friend's answer was simple: "Because it would be better for you."

He then asked me to try to find the good in what had transpired between us and whether my adversary had helped me, even unwittingly. I was puzzled. What good could have come from it all? However, as I reflected more in the days that followed, I realized I had learned an awful lot from this person during the years we worked together. He was an astute businessman, and I had been able to apply some of what I learned from him in my other business dealings with great success.

He had also played a major role in helping me prove to myself that I could take care of myself under extreme pressure and adversity—something I had doubted previously. And importantly, the encounter had changed the trajectory of my career. I went from being beholden to one individual to enjoying the freedom, independence, and empowerment of being the head of a real estate investment company that acquired and managed properties for myself and a diversified group of investors and partners.

I realized that, as strange as it may seem, this person had provided me with blessings that I could not have received in any other way. The shackles were released; I no longer harbored anger toward him.

I thus found that forgiveness is the best and perhaps only way I can heal my deepest heart wounds, put the past behind me, and enjoy what is truly important and meaningful in my life.

I thus encourage people to try and find the good or positive in the entanglements that stoke their anger and resentment. Did any positive changes result? Did they learn anything meaningful about themselves? Did the experience make them better equipped to deal with future challenges? Did they embark on life paths they otherwise might not have?

I used to find myself getting angry or resentful not because of what someone did to me but because of what I failed to do for myself: set boundaries. It happened so often, I even wrote a poem about it.

INQUIRIES AND REFLECTIONS

- What triggers your strong anger or rage? How does it make you feel and for how long?
- Do you suppress your anger? How does it eventually come out?
- How do you process your anger and resentment?
- Do you ever consider whether you had some part—even a small one—in what evoked your anger? How long does it take to admit to it?

CHAPTER TEN

Waves without Borders

Lines silent too often,
Scribbled in grays, are
Easily trampled by the unwary, until
Only regrets remain.

The haze blinds all, as
We become lost in our yielding,
Wandering into pinball dissonance
Where only our absence is seen.

Shouts screech internal,
Resentment festers unbridled, until
All that was uncomfortably given
Is yanked in EXPLOSION.

Finally marking the lines clear,
Roars from addicts we've spawned
Crook our hands, and
Guilt our minds.

Retrieve your translucent chalk,
Heeding the child's easy claim
"That's mine!"
Setting the record straight—
With nary a missed beat.

Bequeath understanding and care for all, by
Honoring your needs, and
Return from victim's exile
Along your Lines of Peace.

—Daniel A. Miller, "Lines of Peace"

WHEN OTHERS ARE BODY-SURFING close to us, we can protect ourselves by communicating clearly and staying within our own waters. When we don't, we risk colliding with them.

Similarly, when we don't establish personal boundaries in our relationships and life affairs, we allow others to intrude upon our currents, and we end up riding waves without borders. Dissension and resentment easily ensue.

If you're like me, when you don't set appropriate boundaries or limits, you end up accommodating the needs of others at the expense of your own. And in renouncing our own needs and interests, we can easily lose ourselves in the pinball dissonance of conflicted feelings and emotions.

The challenge is striking a proper balance between our sense of duty, responsibility, and compassion to others, and the need to honor our own needs and wants. When we don't, we can easily get lost in our yielding.

Some people go to great extremes to satisfy the perceived needs and desires of others—often with little reward. Not unexpectedly, their devotions can produce just the opposite results that they desire. They end up feeling slighted or not appreciated.

I have learned that the best way to secure my borders from unwanted intrusions of others is by communicating my needs and wants in a clear, thoughtful manner. When I so honor them, they become lines of peace—for both me and others—whether they be family and loved ones, friends, or business associates.

During the COVID pandemic I had to set boundaries with Mitch, a friend who suffered from extreme anxiety. Mitch called and texted me daily during the pandemic. Although he was not a close friend, knowing how challenged he was during that time, I tried to help by lending an attentive ear and offering support and encouragement.

After a few months, however, I began feeling pressured and intruded upon, especially by his early morning calls and multiple texts. On a few occasions, I found myself being abrupt with him, which I regretted. I knew I had reached my limit and feared I might cut him off totally, which I didn't want to do.

I thus decided to share my feelings with Mitch about his constant calls and texts. I candidly told him I was on the verge of no longer taking his calls, which I didn't want to do, and asked that he not call me more than twice a week. Mitch said he understood, confiding that several others were no longer accepting his calls, and he didn't want that to happen with us.

Mitch abided by that arrangement for a few months, but then he began calling and texting daily again. I told him as nicely as I could that he was being intrusive and I would have to block his calls if he continued. He now moderates his calls and texts.

For many years, what made setting boundaries difficult was my tendency to view competing interests or desires as irreconcilable or mutually exclusive—as if the only choice was between my needs and desires and those of others. When I felt there were conflicting currents, I would constantly try to come up with ways to satisfy everyone—except myself. The result most often was inconsistent, contradictory behavior.

But setting reasonable boundaries need not be a matter of choosing between conflicting interests or feeling guilty about taking care of our needs. We are not being selfish or inconsiderate when we thoughtfully express our needs and desires. It's more a matter of finding the right balance between being compassionate and wanting to help others and not renouncing our own needs and interests.

However, dissension can arise when we are unkind or forceful in setting boundaries. Statements or demands such as "Stop. You are crossing my boundary," "Leave me alone," and "I need to set a boundary with you" are antagonistic and divisive. Moreover, such proclamations don't set real boundaries. They are merely precursors to unnecessary resentment. A simple "I won't be able to," "I am unable to right now," or "Let me think about it" is an inoffensive way of setting boundaries.

Importantly, there is no need to justify or explain why we don't want to do or allow something. I used to do that, and that only opened the door to responses challenging or questioning my reasons or offering unsatisfactory solutions to them.

Setting boundaries is also important in the workplace. Workers are often reticent to voice their concerns about being overworked, having to endure poor working conditions, or having to kowtow to overbearing bosses. Conversely, to their detriment, some employers sometimes overaccommodate the needs and desires of their employees. Not expressing and honoring their respective needs and interests easily leads to resentment.

This once happened with a part-time bookkeeper who had been highly recommended by my retiring book-keeper. Because of the good recommendation, I didn't give her my basic bookkeeping test, as had always been my practice. Not long after she began working, she started making some errors and keeping irregular hours. The mistakes were not consequential, and I attributed them to some personal family issues that I later learned she was dealing with. I thus didn't let her know that she needed to be more focused in her work duties and maintain more regular hours to minimize mistakes.

Then she made a costly mistake. Angered, I terminated her services on short notice. She was rightfully resentful for not receiving any advance warning, and I was resentful because I had to bear the brunt of her mistake and also at myself for not setting appropriate boundaries with her.

I also have to be mindful not to set boundaries when none are needed. On occasion, I have felt imposed upon because I thought—incorrectly—that people were asking things of me when they really weren't. I have learned that people's wants may not be what I think or assume them to be and that I shouldn't speculate about their motives or intentions. I am usually wrong when I do. If I am unsure or uncertain about what someone may want of me, I can simply inquire.

Additionally, I try to be clear in expressing my needs and wants. Conflicting currents easily arise when I am unclear or ambiguous in expressing them. Most people are not mind readers and may not know what's important to us. They shouldn't have to guess. As my above poem states, "marking the lines clear" is important. Otherwise, we may be sending mixed signals that can easily be misconstrued, leading to unintentional intrusions.

I now view establishing clear boundaries as a win-win situation. It's better for us, and it's better for others. Situations need not be viewed in terms of either-or or you-or-me. They can just as easily be you *and* me. Being forthright about our needs furthers that. When people understand where we stand on matters, they are given the opportunity to respond or adjust accordingly.

It's true that some people will continue to press or impose upon us even after we clearly express our desires and needs. When that happens, we can simply repeat ourselves. If that still doesn't help, we can always choose to swim in more compatible waters.

In sum, establishing our lines of peace can be best accomplished by honoring and clearly expressing our needs and desires, accepting that we are entitled to have them, and knowing that we are not being selfish, inconsiderate, or harmful to others in doing so.

And for sure, the rides will be smoother.

There is one obstructor that is an undercurrent of most other obstructors: fear.

INQUIRIES AND REFLECTIONS

- How comfortable are you telling someone "I can't" or "I'd appreciate your not doing that"? Do you feel the need to explain why?
- Do you feel selfish giving priority to your own needs? Does your priority change depending on the nature of your relationship with the other person?
- How do you balance and set boundaries between your work and personal affairs?
- Do you ever feel taken advantage of by your boss or employer? How can you change that?

CHAPTER ELEVEN

Fearful Currents

A master of disguise
With tentacles so long,
Flourishing like wild mint
In the tepid soil of our minds.

With us unbeknownst
Its heavy silence so loud, it
Feeds our anxiety, and
Nourishes only our doubts.

Deceit's best lover.
So blindfold brave,
Sharks our dreams,
Tons our creativity.

Yet . . . truly a coward until unmasked
    Stare its stare,
        Deflect its glare,
            Strip it bare.

Reveal this thing FEAR
For what it truly is,
A wimp hiding in our frail armor
Parading as Fiction's Best Seller.

—Daniel A. Miller, "Fiction's Best Seller"

WHEN WE ARE AFRAID of waves, we are overly cautious when riding them, bypass the best ones to ride, or feel reluctant to ride them at all.

Similarly, our unprocessed fears prevent us from engaging and aligning with such life currents as work and finances, problematic relationships, and health and self-care, among others. Our vision is impaired by worries and speculations mainly about future currents that haven't arrived or may never.

It was no coincidence that my learning to ride the Wave correlated with my learning to *lose* fear or at least defuse it considerably. When I could *lose* fear, I could *lose* control, and when I could *lose* control, I could *find* flow.

People say that courage overcomes fear, as does faith and prayer. We should encourage whatever means that can assist us in reducing or overcoming our fears to help us navigate our life currents. I view it as a two-step process: We first need to identify our fears. We then need to process them.

Detecting fear can be tricky because it often basks in our ignorance; it is a master of disguise. We may attribute our anger, discomfort, or anxiety to other things, not realizing that the source is primarily fear.

As I shared in *Losing Control, Finding Serenity*, I wasn't in touch with my fears for many months following the breakup of my first marriage. I was stoic and expressed little emotion and found myself unable to get in touch with my grief and sadness. My respite was to dive into work, where I felt I had more control over things. This reaction was mainly a diversionary tactic. Only later when I got in touch with my fear of being alone and the uncertainty about the future was I able to release the heaviness within me.

One of the best ways I found to detect this most tricky of emotions is to do what I call a fear inquiry. When I feel unsettled, anxious, or depressed, I take a moment to think about what I might be afraid of. Maybe nothing comes up at first. But if I push a little deeper or look for signs, such as shortness of breath, a tightened chest, or lethargy, I might find the answer.

Because my nature is to block discomfiting feelings, I try to recall the day's or week's events specifically. The fear-invoking event is usually lurking in there somewhere. It may have been too painful to deal with initially, so I creatively deflected it. I used to block adverse circumstances for weeks at a time until they finally manifested themselves in strong physical reactions.

As I mentioned earlier, procrastination and avoidance are usually signs of an underlying fear. This was evident during the financial crisis following the bank's calling of my loans. Many times, I literally couldn't lift the phone to make the necessary calls to ask other banks for funding. It wasn't until I could pinpoint and process (a method I'll explain below) the gripping fear of financial collapse that I was able to move forward.

Once I have a clearer understanding of my fears, I next try to process them, which is to say I lean in or move closer to—even embrace—them. As I listen to the concerns and apprehensions embedded in my fears, I try to stay in the moment with whatever truths are revealed. This practice can be very unsettling and, in its own way frightening because I am touching my innermost truths and vulnerability.

I also try to feel the fear physically and note where it resides in my body—my chest, stomach, back, or somewhere else. I inhale slowly and deeply through my nose, drawing my breath down to my navel and feeling the physical sensations—usually a vibration or current-like sensation—then exhale slowly. After a few minutes of such breathing, I feel more grounded, and that alone weakens my fear's grip over me. Fears don't like being examined too closely; their bark is much worse than their bite.

Sometimes I will share my fears with a confidant or trusted person—usually my wife. Just getting them out in the open is relieving. My wife often points out options I might not have considered or information I might have misperceived or misconstrued. Her simple reassurances that everything will be okay help considerably.

Processing fears in these manners places them in reality by separating fact from fiction. It rids the mind of all the what-ifs and what-might-happens and replaces them with what-is-real-nows. I can then take actions or steps to address the underlying reality.

Most of my fears and concerns are based mainly on suppositions, speculations, and assumptions—usually negative—about events or circumstances that haven't yet occurred or inaccurate or incomplete information. And more often than not, the dreaded events never end up occurring, or at least not in the way I had imagined, or the facts turned out to be much different than I had assumed.

Two acronyms for FEAR make processing fears easier: "future events already ruined" and "false evidence appearing real." Just repeating these acronyms aloud weakens my fear's hold. Ipso facto, nothing in the future can be ruined in this exact moment.

Ralph Waldo Emerson expressed this folly in sweet verse:

Some of your hurts you have cured,
And the sharpest you still have survived,
But what torments of grief you've endured,
From evils which never arrived![1]

Seneca, the Roman stoic philosopher and playwright, also offered some perspective: "Many are harmed by fear itself, and many have come to their fate while dreading fate."[2]

When you are dealing with unabated fear and anxiety—the kind that keeps you up all night for days on end—a worst-case scenario exercise can help. The psychologist William Duff taught this to me during my financial crisis when things were the bleakest. I had been having nightmares about unsavory people chasing me and finding myself in precarious situations with no seeming way out.   Here's how the session went:

Dr. Duff: What would be the worst thing that could happen to you if you are unable to repay your bank loans?

Me: My credit would be shot and the bank would sue me.

Dr. Duff: What would happen then?

Me: The bank would obtain a judgment against me and attach my assets.

Dr. Duff: What then?

Me: I would be broke and out of business!

Dr. Duff: And?

Me (smiling): I would have nothing to do but lie on the beach all day.

What a pleasant thing to do as a worst case. Far different from the foreboding images my imagination had conned me into believing. I thus faced my deepest fears and gained proper perspective of my situation, and the tensions and anxiety immediately left. A short time later, I persuaded another bank to loan me enough money to pay off my loan and then some extra for my business recovery. I had called fear's bluff, and that's exactly what it was—a bluff.

I have since discovered many times over that when I identify and process my fears, they run their course and dissipate by themselves, much like a current of water running along the street curb does after it stops raining. The tentacles of my fears loosen their grip, and I find immediate relief. They are less daunting. I am able to strip away whatever fantasies my mind is so adept at scripting when as my poem above states, I "Stare its stare, / Deflect its glare, / Strip it bare."

Notably, the obstructors we have thus far looked at relate mainly to what we perceive as others doing to us or what we do to ourselves. The next chapter looks at one that seems to linger somewhere in between: lulls.

INQUIRIES AND REFLECTIONS

- How do you identify and process your fears? Do they become less daunting?
- How often do your biggest fears come to fruition? When they do, are they as bad as you had imagined or speculated?
- Do you worry too much about future outcomes? How can you avoid that?
- Are you more controlling when you are fearful?

CHAPTER TWELVE

Lull Tides

Sit in reverie and watch the changing color of the
waves that break upon the idle seashore of the
mind.

—Henry Wadsworth Longfellow

CONTINUOUS LOW-BREAKING WAVES CLOSE to shore are
not a body-surfer's delight! A body-surfer who faces these
conditions must either linger in the water for an indefi-
nite period waiting for better waves to arrive or just go
home and surf another day.

I feel the same way when I'm in a lull. Not much
is happening, and nothing really interests me. I'm just
biding time and feeling uncomfortable about not doing
anything productive and wondering, "What should I do
now?" Even the word *lull* brings on a certain dread.

I've noticed that my lulls usually occur after I've
completed an activity or endeavor in which I was actively
engaged, particularly if it was enjoyable and gratifying. I
experienced such a lull after the five years of writing *The
Gifts of Acceptance.* I was excited and deeply gratified that the
book garnered good reviews, received some book awards,
and became an Amazon bestseller in multiple categories and
even more so when readers expressed how much the book
had helped them with their acceptance issues.

A couple months after the book release, I suddenly had a lot of time on my hands. I've never been good with too much time on my hands. I get antsy not knowing what to do. I also feel lethargic and have less energy, even on the tennis court playing the game I love. For a while, I pondered whether I should write another book or start painting again, which had taken a backseat to my writing in recent years. But truth be told, I had no real desire to do either—at least not then.

What helped bring me out of the doldrums was the realization that I had a bad case of denial. I would be turning seventy-six in a couple of months, and my stinking thinking kept reminding me that eighty was just around the corner—and that didn't feel good at all.

I half-jokingly told my wife that I must have bypassed a midlife crisis and am now having a late life one. She offered some sage advice: practice gratitude.

It's easy to lose sight of all the good things in our lives when we are not feeling up to par. There's an imbalance that needs correcting, and focusing on our blessings helps us do that. It can be as simple as counting our blessings. For me, that includes being grateful for my caring family and friends, a comfortable home, my good health, and my financial security—and doing so daily. I sometimes vocalize or write them down.

An enlightening exercise is to write down one hundred things you are grateful for, without judging their significance. It's surprising how many gifts we lose sight of. In making such a list during my book lull, I realized that seventy-six was just a number, and it didn't define who I was or limit me. Only I had the power to do that. That realization released the unease I was feeling considerably.

Having time on my hands—as lulls tend to provide—one day, I decided to box and move some of my old files to a storage shed we have in our rear yard. I came across fifteen chapters of an earlier version of a book on the Wave that I had penned in 1988. I hadn't finished the book because I didn't then know or understand enough about the way of the Wave—particularly its obstructors and enhancers—to articulate the concept well. Several months later, I began writing this very book.

Through this experience, I learned that lulls are obstructors only if we choose to make them so. They can be peaceful. They can be informative. And they can be revealing. Lulls can be viewed as do-nothing, bland, going nowhere waves that are later followed by colorful, inspiring, exhilarating ones. We just need to be patient, trusting, and open to what the currents bring us.

In the meantime, we can do activities and tasks that we didn't have time to do before or that we kept putting off. Paring down, going through old photos, getting rid of unneeded and little-used personal items, being out in nature more, enjoying creative activities, volunteering, and spending more time with family are just some of the benefits of lulls.

Like many others, I experienced long lulls during the COVID-19 pandemic. Every day seemed the same, yet I felt different almost daily. The days felt the same in the sense that I had a lot of time on my hands and was restricted in movement, engagement, and enjoyment of what I like to do, especially playing tennis. And they seemed different in the sense that I didn't know how I would feel until I got out of bed and began my day. On the better days, I was relaxed and made good use of the extra time I had. On other days, time dragged with nothing to do.

Reaching out to friends to see how they were doing helped a lot. It wasn't always easy because a lot of the time I wasn't in the mood to speak to anyone. But I knew from experience that one of the best ways to get away from my negative thoughts was to lend a good ear to others, especially those who were struggling during the pandemic. My friends uniformly welcomed me warmly. We shared what we were doing with our extra time and had some good laughs. These conversations lightened my spirit considerably.

I often immersed myself in nature. In California, we have so much natural beauty all around us and being in its midst was uplifting and grounding. I'd walk along the beach or hike mountain trails, take evening strolls in our neighborhood, smell the roses, and look at the irises blooming brightly and the blue sky getting bluer from the lack of cars on the road. And I couldn't help noticing that the birds' medleys were more cheerful than ever. Even the gentle doves looked more peaceful.

I also explored ways in which practicing acceptance could normalize my life by lessening concerns and anxiety in the midst of great uncertainty during that period. At the suggestion of my eldest daughter, I wrote a series of blog posts about the tools and strategies that helped me achieve greater serenity during the pandemic. (I later compiled them into an e-book guide, *Acceptance in the Time of COVID-19*, that is available for no cost at danielamiller.com.)

I was careful not to fall into the something-must-be-wrong-with-me trap. Nothing is wrong with us when we are having lulls. Life will always have ups and downs—and lulls—and they pass sooner when we lean into our uncomfortable feelings and get in touch with any emptiness, unproductiveness, or boredom that we may be feeling.

I have a friend who upon retiring from an incredibly active, responsible job dealing with the impact of carbon emissions on the climate suddenly had a lot of time on his hands and was not sure what to do with it. He shared that he was doing a lot of soul searching about the future. Sensing his concerns, I offered that he was simply having a lull. Hearing that term, his energy perked up. "Yes," he said, "I'm having a lull. That's what it is." It seemed to ease his concerns.

I remember the words offered by a therapist when I was at the low point of my travails many years ago: "Danny, what a wonderful opportunity." I was taken aback upon first hearing her words. But she was right. I had an opportunity to change my counterproductive ways and move in a different direction: upward. And that's what I did. I thus encourage people to view lulls as opportunities to expand their life currents.

As we've seen, wave obstructors are powerful deterrents to riding the Wave and navigating our life currents. Fortunately, there are equally impactful wave enhancers that facilitate the flow. The next chapter looks at one that effectively counters most obstructors: trust.

INQUIRIES AND REFLECTIONS

- What feelings do lulls stir up for you? Do they cause you to judge or question where you are at in your life?

- Do you keep busy just to keep busy? Is it difficult for you to just be?

- Do you equate lulls with being in ruts? Why or why not?

- What things did you accomplish during your pandemic lulls that you didn't have time for before?

PART THREE

Wave Enhancers

CHAPTER THIRTEEN

Trusting the Flow

No matter how hard the waves are, you will float
on the ocean.

—Kubbra Sait

HOWEVER THE WAVES BREAK and whatever the water's
condition, experienced body-surfers have learned to trust
that they can make the adjustments necessary to ensure
their safety and well-being and still have enjoyable rides.

Not long ago, at a get-together with some friends, one
shared that what helps him most in dealing with life's ups
and downs is his belief that "It's going to be okay. It may not
be what I wanted or expected, and I may not like it, but it's
going to be okay." It was his way of saying that he trusted he
would be able to handle whatever may occur in his life.

My friend's comment resonated with me. In recent
years, trusting my life currents has enhanced my
life in so many ways. Simply put, it makes life easier.
Trust effectively counters fear, limited thinking, high
expectations, and the need to control.

That certainly wasn't always the case for me. As a
controller, fear and worry left little space for trust. Even in
my tennis matches, trust was absent for many years. As a
senior tennis player, I had struggled to play up to my ability

in tournament match play. I was constantly overthinking and too cautious and concerned about making errors. Consequently, I struggled to get into the flow of the match. I didn't trust that if I just let go and didn't concern myself about the outcomes, such as the score or where the ball went, I would make good shots. In other words, I didn't trust my game, which is to say myself.

Then one year before playing in a popular tournament in Palm Springs, I read a statement about trusting my game in Jeff Greenwald's insightful book, *The Best Tennis of Your Life*, that really resonated with me: "Letting go of control, trusting your shots, and accepting the outcome is imperative if you are going to ever play with true freedom on the court."[1]

Following that advice in the tournament, I defeated several players who had soundly beat me the year before, before losing in a close match to the number one seed in the semifinals. By trusting that my body and mind can work things out without all my "help," I have since ridden the tennis Wave to greater success and enjoyment on the courts. My mantra on the court now is "Trust. Just trust."

One of the telltale signs that I'm not trusting the flow is when I start developing a sense of urgency. It can surface in simple, everyday ways, such as when I am running around doing errands or taking care of personal needs. It happens a lot when my workload spikes. I begin worrying that I may not have enough time to take care of everything and lose perspective and a sense of my priorities. To help me, I placed a sticky note on my computer that says, "How urgent is it?"

I have become more aware of the strong link between trust and fear and anxiety. When I am not trusting, it's most often because I am anxious or fearful about something, and when I am trusting, I have much less fear and anxiety. And certainly, when I trust, I am more at ease.

Simple mathematics suggests we are better served by trusting the flow when encountering uncertain or unknown waters. An example is when my friend Ryan called one evening all frazzled. His car's warning light had gone on as he reached home, and he was worrying obsessively that he wouldn't have enough money if a major repair was required when his mechanic inspected his car the next day.

In an effort to ease his concern, I said, "Let's assume that there's a 50 percent chance your car will require only a minor repair and a 50 percent chance that it will require a major repair, all things being equal. Why not trust that the outcome will be positive? If you don't, you will worry and be anxious until the outcome is known the next day, and if it turns out that only a minor repair is needed, wouldn't all your worry and anxiety—and the energy expended—have been for naught?"

Ryan concurred. I continued: "Conversely, if you trust that the outcome would be positive—a minor repair—and it later turned out that a major repair was required, then your worry and anxiety needn't begin until it was known the next day. That's a lot of saved worry and anxiety. And your anxiety would likely be less since you could take steps to deal with the problem at the most propitious time: when the outcome was known." Fortunately for Ryan, the warning light went off when he started his car the next morning, and no repairs were required!

Here's another way to look at it: most outcomes are just as likely to be positive as negative, so why not put our mental energy into trusting that everything will be okay until the outcome is known instead of expending it on worrisome speculations?

Being mindful of this reduces my worry in more important situations, such as waiting for the results of medical tests or a procedure, how a child's job review will go, readers' responses to a new book, and a myriad of other unknowns.

The practice also works well in my real estate business, where market unknowns and uncertainties are common and there appear to be no clear courses or directions. Typical of this is a commercial property of mine that has been occupied by a prominent pet retailer for fifteen years but whose lease was due to expire in a couple of years. I had continually debated and worried about whether I should sell the property because of the uncertainty as to whether the tenant would renew its lease. With my overly analytical mind, I could list at least five reasons to keep it and five reasons to sell it. The scale never seemed to tip one way or the other. In short, the investment waters were murky.

I decided to test the waters by putting the property up for sale and see what happened. There was little interest. After I lowered the price several times, still without much buyer interest, it became apparent that the risks in keeping the property were the same as the ones that deterred buyers from purchasing it. With only a few years remaining on the lease, who would want to risk owning an empty building if the tenant didn't renew its lease?

Because I wasn't ready for a garage sale, I decided to just tread water and trust that things would work out okay one way or the other. I stopped worrying about what I should do and focused on matters that I had more control over, such as improving the operations of my other properties.

Two years later, the COVID-19 tidal wave struck, and store closures became the norm. After the initial deluge, pet stores began to thrive. Pet owners cared about the well-being of their pets. Additionally, many people wanted company in their pandemic-imposed solitude, and what better way than with loving animals. Pet adoptions, especially for dogs, skyrocketed, as did pet store businesses. Many more animals needed to be fed and cared for.

I was of course lucky and am extremely grateful in having a tenant that was impacted only initially by the pandemic. At the same time, though, had I not trusted the currents as I did, I could have made a precipitous decision instead of waiting for clearer waters. Those waters arrived two years later when the tenant extended its lease for ten more years.

This is not to say that we shouldn't plan and prepare for potential riptides. We should. Nor should we adapt a laissez-faire, carefree attitude in which we just let the cards fall where they may. We shouldn't.

Importantly, trust is not a passive mindset. We can plan and be proactive. But dwelling or speculating on the negative doesn't benefit anyone. In general, I think a good mantra is "Trust—don't speculate."

At the same time, it's not as simple as just turning on a trust switch. As a controller for most of my adult life, I didn't have that switch. This is likely the case for most controllers and micromanagers, who feel they need to know where their currents are headed. For them, uncertain outcomes are to be feared, for who knows what sea creatures may be lurking in the waters.

Basic trust reminders or affirmations can help when a person is apprehensive about outcomes. Here are some that I use:

- "Trust."
- "Everything will be okay."
- "Let it go."
- "Don't speculate."
- "Don't overthink things."
- "I don't have to decide right now."
- "Don't press."
- "It doesn't have to get done today."

Ultimately, trust is about having faith that we will be secure wherever our currents take us.

The next chapter looks at an enhancer that goes hand in hand with trust: humility.

INQUIRIES AND REFLECTIONS

- Do you trust that you can handle most of your challenges?
- How much of a role does trust play in your job or career, in your parenting, or when dealing with uncertainty?
- Do you believe there is a link between trust and fear? What about trust and anxiety or trust and serenity?
- How do you balance trust and taking risks?

CHAPTER FOURTEEN

Navigating Humbly

A man wrapped up in himself makes a very small
bundle.

—Attributed to Benjamin Franklin

EVEN THE MOST CONFIDENT and fearless of body-surfers
are mindful of remaining humble when riding waves. If
they are brash or overconfident, they can take serious
spills. Similarly, when we are arrogant or self-righteous
or have an inflated ego in engaging with people and situations, we can tarnish relationships and outcomes.

I often tell the story of how I pressured my youngest
daughter, who was in middle school at the time, to adopt
the same study habits that had been successful for me in
school: take good class notes, study in a quiet area, sit
up straight, and prepare well in advance for upcoming
exams. As a controller, I didn't hesitate to ask her to do
the same many times over. To my chagrin, she continued
to do things differently. She took few notes, listened to
loud music while studying, usually studied while reclined
in her bed, and always waited until the last minute before
cramming for important tests.

To say the least, in my father-knows-best mode, I
had trouble accepting her study habits. On one telling

occasion, when she was twelve years old, I pressured her to begin studying for her finals well in advance of the test dates. She looked up at me and without missing a beat responded:

"Daddy, I can't do it that way. I'm different from you, and I process things differently. Listening to loud music helps me study better, and I need a sense of urgency to concentrate."

I was immediately taken aback by her truth. My daughter truly is different from me—vastly so. She budgets her time differently, prioritizes differently, has different interests and talents, and has difficulty focusing for extended periods of time. Yet none of these realities stopped her from consistently receiving good grades throughout her schooling and graduating with high honors in college.

Through that encounter, I had a strong reckoning: I didn't know what was best for my loved ones—or others—and I was not nearly as humble as I liked to believe. I may have been mild mannered and soft-spoken, but I definitely wasn't humble. If anything, I was arrogant and self-righteous in not understanding that every person is unique and responds to events and challenges differently.

Who am I to say that my way is the best way—for my daughter or anyone else? My way is just a way, nothing more. Just because something works or has worked well for me doesn't mean it will also work well for others. I know I don't like it when other people tell me what is best for me or what I should do. Unless I ask for their input, I rarely do what they propose. I strongly believe that people have their own life path and are entitled to make the choices and decisions that influence and ultimately determine their path unless I or those whom I care for might be harmed.

In terms of the Wave, this means honoring that everyone has their own currents and is entitled to navigate them without my interference, unless they undermine mine.

This fundamental belief has enabled me to accept my children and loved ones as they are and to serve them best as a supporter, confidant, and, at times, mentor and protector. In doing so, I have been privileged to both enjoy and learn from their unique attributes and talents. They have been my greatest teachers in many respects.

Embedded in humility is an interesting paradox. I have found that when I press or tell others what I think is best for them, they are more likely to resist or be dismissive. And when I refrain from doing so, they often end up doing what I would have suggested. Moreover, they were more committed to their decision because it was theirs, not mine.

However, even knowing these things, I am not as humble as I would like to be. My ego-based mindset often takes over when I am worried or anxious about something or somebody or just closed-minded. In fact, one day as I was working on this very chapter, my wife came into my office and said I should start my car to charge the battery because it had been sitting awhile in the garage. I responded in my typical know-it-all-ness that it wasn't necessary. I wish I had been more humble! When I went to start the car a few days later, the battery was dead, and I had to buy a new one.

I thus need to constantly rein in that part of me that thinks "I know what's best for him—and need to let him know" or "She's doing it all wrong." I also need to be mindful that others' points of view and choices have validity for them.

The following reminders help moderate these propensities:

- "Live and let live."
- "I don't know what's best for others."
- "They are not me, and I am not them."
- "Every person has his or her own path."
- "There is more than one right way."
- "If I'm humble, I won't stumble."

At my core, I must remain teachable and be open to alternative perceptions of reality, as well as be kind and respectful. When I am humble, I am conveying that, in my eyes, others are good and able enough, that I honor their right to make their own choices, and that I am allowing them the dignity of learning from their mistakes. These are empowering gifts—for them and me. People feel safer in opening up and sharing their concerns with me and on occasion even asking for my advice.

Trusting the currents and navigating humbly are enhanced when we follow the path of truth, as explained in the next chapter.

INQUIRIES AND REFLECTIONS

- Do you consider yourself to be a humble person? What attributes do you feel make you so?

- How much do you advise or pressure your children or others to do things the way you do or did?

- Do you see any connection between humility and limited thinking or humility and being open-minded?

- Do you recognize the inverse relationship between humility and control and humility and judgment?

CHAPTER FIFTEEN

Truthful Rides

Three things cannot long be hidden: the sun, the moon, and the truth.

—Anna Voigt and Nevill Drury

WHETHER WAVES ORIGINATE FROM the energy created by the wind blowing over water or the ocean bottom causing waves to rise and pitch forward, the movement of waves holds an innate truth—an "as-is-ness." When body-surfers align with the waves as they are, the rides will be safer and smoother even in turbulent water. When they don't, rough rides usually lie ahead.

In a similar manner, when we engage and navigate our life currents in a candid, truthful manner, life is easier. When we don't, we snake through winding currents that create conflict and dissension and plant the seeds of separation, ones in which trust is damaged and not easily restored and that consume inordinate amounts of time and energy.

Simply put, truth and candor make it easier to navigate our life currents. Truth enhances the flow; dishonesty and deception disrupt it. Hence, when family or friends ask for my advice on what they should say or do when dealing with troublesome situations or dilemmas, my answer is two words: "Be truthful."

Even when being truthful is met with anger or resentment, these reactions tend to be more muted than when we aren't. That's because truth diffuses and softens the pain; deceit fuels and exacerbates it. I noticed this dynamic when I counseled investors about their failed real estate investments. Many had not received full information when they invested or had been misinformed about their investment's performance. Most were angry and some were vindictive when they learned the true facts. Most were more understanding and forgiving of adversity when offered truth and transparency.

When a couple of my own real estate investments soured, I had to disclose—albeit with discomfort—the bad news to my partners and ask them for additional funds to keep the properties afloat. They weren't happy. However, most were appreciative of my being up front, and some invested with me again.

Most people know that everything is not a bed of roses. They want to know where the thorns are so they can evaluate the risks and better protect themselves against getting pricked.

That includes family. In my early twenties, when my beloved grandfather had incurable cancer, my family decided not to disclose it to him. They were concerned that he would give up hope and deteriorate more quickly. We thus kept up the facade that he was going to get better. Worse yet, as he weakened, we had to come up with false explanations as to why he was not getting better.

We all lost by that decision, and I deeply regret my part in it. By denying my grandfather the truth, we deprived him of the dignity to face his disease with acceptance and grace and the opportunity to share fond memories and last wishes with us. Toward the end, he knew he had been misled and was placed in the unbearable position of having to play along with our facade. (A close friend of his revealed that to me years later.) To this day, I mourn not only my grandfather's loss but also not being able to share some final intimate moments with him.

So-called half-truths and white lies can also impede the flow. Sometimes we don't want to hurt others' feelings or make them feel bad, but small falsehoods can multiply and later divide when discovered.

Navigating truthfully also encompasses honoring our inner truths. Almost every day, we experience a wide range of feelings, many unwanted, that impact us emotionally, physically, and spiritually. These feelings are our intrinsic personal truths. They are the real us—our heart and soul— shed of facades, defenses, and justifications. They include our shame, guilt, grief, sadness, failures, and insecurities. These feelings are often masked and suppressed as we become engulfed in our daily storms. When not processed, they hinder our ability to accurately read the currents. We see dark clouds rather than blue skies.

Awareness is an important first step in addressing these uncomfortable feelings. I try to repress the urge to quickly push through them by pausing to notice when I feel somehow off or not right. These feelings need to be acknowledged and let out. Taking some deep breaths allows me to get better in touch with what is happening internally. I check for any discomforts or physical symptoms, even if I don't know their cause.

Once I become more aware of these feelings, I try to lean into them regardless of how uncomfortable or vulnerable it makes me feel. These feelings are part of me—many with a long history—and I try not to judge or think of them (or myself) as good or bad but rather that they exist and deserve my attention.

At its heart, this practice is a personal exploration of the ways that enable us to connect with our soul center. There is no set of rules. The key is to directly face and process our truths. Even making partial headway helps considerably. Below are some ways that have helped me and others get better in touch with these feelings. They are by no means exclusive and are not intended to limit your personal explorations:

Prayer—Prayers for understanding, guidance, and courage to face our challenges help. As stated earlier, I say the Serenity Prayer every day upon waking, for acceptance and guidance.

Centering practice—I also take a few moments at intervals during the day to get in touch with how I am feeling. Sometimes I meditate or do deep-breathing exercises to still my mind and gain clarity. I may stretch or go outside for a while and listen to cheerful birds, take a short walk, or just breathe in the fresh air. Just being in nature can be comforting and revealing.

Daily exercise—For me, playing tennis, jogging, going to the gym, or swimming helps take the edge off things and uncover truths.

Religion or spiritual practices—Many people find religion instrumental in processing their inner truths, whether it be through prayer, traditional religious services and rituals, or the counsel of religious leaders within their community. Many others rely on spiritual practices such as meditation and visualization.

If I had to pinpoint what seems to be inherent in all these practices, it is the fostering of a stillness and calmness that quiets the incessant chatter of our minds, connects us with our soul center, and grounds us in the present—where our real truths reside. That is where alignment with our life currents most naturally occurs.

Another benefit of honoring our personal truths is that it maximizes a wave enhancer that guides us toward better choices and decisions: intuition.

INQUIRIES AND REFLECTIONS

- Does your commitment to the truth lessen when the stakes are higher?
- Does your being truthful vary depending on whether the person is a family member, friend, coworker, or acquaintance? Why or why not?
- How do you process your inner truths?
- How do you respond when people aren't truthful with you?

CHAPTER SIXTEEN

Intuitive Navigations

Listen to the sound of waves within you.

—Rumi

AS BODY-SURFERS GAIN EXPERIENCE in riding waves, their instincts and intuition play an increasingly larger role in selecting the best ones to ride and how to ride them.

Likewise, trusting our intuition plays a major role in making good choices and decisions, especially when matters are unclear, outcomes are uncertain, or not all pertinent facts are known.

A common definition of intuition is the acquiring of knowledge without recourse to conscious reasoning. Albert Einstein explained its essence more fully: "The intellect has little to do on the road to discovery. There comes a leap in consciousness, call it intuition or what you will, and the solution comes to you, and you don't know how or why." Sri Daya Mata, spiritual head of the Self-Realization Center in Los Angeles for fifty years, referred to intuition as "soul guidance for life decisions."[1]

My dad always referred to it as "listening to that little person inside." Others think of it as following their instincts or gut feeling. However one may think of it, our intuition is adept at integrating diverse facts, information, and factors with past experiences to make better choices and decisions.

We often have to solve or resolve life puzzles in which the pieces seem to be from different boxes or some pieces are missing. Our minds can easily be taxed in trying to assign relative importance to countervailing factors and considerations. I believe that our intuitions serve as a master calculator that takes them into account in a way that better aligns us with our life currents.

For example, we may need to weigh the financial consequences of working fewer hours versus the joy of having more time to pursue our interests and passions. Or we may need to reduce business expenses during a weakening economy and decide which employee to let go or reduce hours for: a hardworking, loyal one with average skills or a highly skilled employee who doesn't collaborate well with his or her fellow workers.

Or we may, like I did, be struggling about whether to make repairs to a leaky roof at a moderate cost, but with no assurance of how long the roof will hold up, or to spend considerably more to replace the roof and gain the benefit of a ten-year warranty.

I most often rely on my intuition in determining whether, when, or how to take or not take certain actions. For example, I go with my gut feeling on whether I can trust or rely on someone to handle something important, how much information I should disclose to someone, when would be a good time to discuss a sensitive issue with someone, or how to handle a prickly situation.

Once, just as I was about to send an email forcefully responding to someone's heated accusation, something in me said, "Wait! Don't do anything right now." When

I reread the email the next morning, I shortened it and changed its tone considerably before sending it.

In my real estate business, I rely on my intuition in deciding whether and to whom to rent space. Thus, while prospective tenants' credit and financial condition are important factors, sometimes I will pick up on the way people express themselves, how transparent they are, or the compatibility of their business operations with other tenants and decide to rent to a financially weaker tenant.

In today's tech world, where important nuance can easily be lost in communications, I rely on my intuition to determine whether it would be better to text, email, call, or meet with the person.

Delving further, I have thought about what factors typically influence my intuitive responses. They include people's facial expressions, tones of voice, and word choices or vibes they've conveyed. Other factors are their demeanor or how they present themselves, their experiences and history, or other cues, many of them subliminal.

Ultimately, I believe our intuition works best when we are centered and have addressed any unwanted feelings, such as fear, anger, anxiety, and frustration. While assessing and evaluating our choices are prudent steps, when we overthink and overanalyze, our mental energy can easily get sapped, leaving little space for our intuition to intuit.

There is one enhancer that plays a dual role in productively navigating our life currents by giving us the mental and physical health and well-being to counter the obstructors and more fully embrace the other enhancers: self-care.

INQUIRIES AND REFLECTIONS

- How do you think of intuition? How much do you rely on it?

- In what kinds of situations do you find it most beneficial?

- How much do past experiences impact your intuition?

- Do you distinguish between instinct and intuition? In which way?

CHAPTER SEVENTEEN

Self-Caring Currents

Self-love, my liege, is not so vile a sin as self-neglecting.

—William Shakespeare

WHEN BODY-SURFERS SPEND TOO much time riding waves, they become tired, depleted, and out of sync with the flow of the waves. This puts them at risk of serious harm.

In a similar manner, when we are consumed with navigating our life currents—particularly ones involving work, finances, and caring for others—to the exclusion of other waves, we neglect to take proper care of ourselves. Emotional, physical, and spiritual harm easily ensue. It is critical to take proper care of ourselves so that we can navigate our life currents to the fullest.

A parable here is apropos: A man owned a very special car—one with smooth, clean lines that drove like a dream. Few cars on the road could match it. In the beginning, the man took meticulously good care of his car. He always hand-washed and waxed it, serviced it on a consistent schedule, and kept it covered. As he became busier and busier at work in dealing with urgent matters, he missed some of the car's scheduled checkups and didn't cover it all the time. And to save time, he began taking the car to a regular car wash where it would sometimes get little nicks. Eventually, he stopped washing the car on any regular basis.

Not surprisingly, the car began driving in a sporadic, unreliable manner, almost as if it couldn't muster the energy it once had. Still preoccupied with his work struggles, the man decided he needed a more reliable car, so he purchased a new one, but it had no special flair.

As if offended, the older car's engine sputtered more and more until one day, it suddenly died. The man couldn't believe what had happened. Even though he knew he had neglected the car, he felt it was still strong and fit enough to keep running.

I was that man and that was my special car. Not only did my dream car break down, I did too. I learned the hard way about not taking proper care of myself. As mentioned earlier, I ended up losing half my nose because of neglect. I cancelled multiple doctor appointments for a simple office procedure and later ended up in the hospital with multiple major surgeries. I feared that if I called time-out from my urgent work duties, something ominous would happen to me. Well, it did—from neglecting my health care.

My fear had run rampant. When my bank unexpectedly called my loans, I believed that if I didn't devote all my time to finding a way to repay them, the bank would sick its bloodhounds on me in the form of attaching my bank accounts, reporting me to credit agencies, and suing me. It felt as if I might be pulled down from behind, as if I were a deer that an alligator grabbed just as the prey animal was about to climb out of the river or, in my case, just as I was making headway in securing a replacement loan from another bank.

I was without question justified in feeling the pressure of my mounting debt that bore 21 percent interest. Yet my fear and lack of any sense of proportionality, far more than was realistic, caused me to cancel the medical appointments. The reality was that I could have taken several hours off to visit the doctor—hours in which I was more often than not engaged in that useless mental activity commonly known as *worrying*. Had I known about the way of the Wave then, I don't doubt that I would now have a much nicer looking nose.

The irony is that self-neglect deters us from achieving the very things for which we strive. As I did, we may believe that taking the time to care for ourselves could doom our efforts. Yet only through proper self-care are we likely to achieve those things.

For example, if we have to deal with an important personal or business matter or situation when physically tired or mentally exhausted, we will likely not feel confident and focused enough to produce a positive outcome. On the other hand, if we are fit, rested, and clear minded, we will be more alert and focused and have a greater likelihood of success.

How can we begin riding self-care currents that lead to emotional, physical, and spiritual well-being? While the specific ways are likely different for each of us, I believe two interlinked truths are integral to the endeavor:

- A life without self-care is a life out of balance.

- A life out of balance often leads to emotional, physical, and spiritual ill health.

My life had been clearly out of balance. That's what brought me to the beach that day many years ago. It started becoming more balanced as I learned the way of the Wave—more specifically, as I progressed in reducing its obstructors and practicing its enhancers. With less fear, anger, anxiety, judgment, and limitations and more trust, acceptance, and awareness, self-care eventually became a natural part of my daily routine.

In particular, losing control—first at work, then in my personal affairs—freed a lot of time.[1] Controlling behaviors, including hovering, directing, pressing, intimidating, and manipulating, are time-consuming and energy depleting. Many of them are unproductive and even wasted time. Letting go of control also freed new currents that were often more time efficient. Practicing acceptance—of people, places, things, and situations—saved even more time, since I was not trying to change them.

Consequently, losing control and practicing acceptance not only freed up enough time in which to care for my personal needs, it also gave me time to enjoy my passions of painting, writing, and playing tennis.

However, even with more time available, I had to overcome the barrier of self-judgment—the uncomfortable feeling that I was being self-indulgent if I tended to my personal needs too much. I am not sure whether that belief was derived from my upbringing or other reasons, but it existed. Whatever the cause, I now consider it a duty to take good care of myself.

Nonetheless, I can fall back into self-neglect if I am not aware of its signs. To this day, if my car is dirty or unkempt, it's a telltale sign that I am neglecting more than just my car. Other indications include not getting a timely haircut or allowing excessive clutter to build up in my office. I will definitely no longer miss a doctor's appointment.

In the beginning, to create more awareness, I made a personal to-do list on Sunday evenings or first thing Monday mornings and placed it on my desk next to my business to-do list, which, as a Virgo organizer and controller, I had always maintained. I also carried a copy of the list around with me for ready access. I set aside portions of certain days to do one or two things on the list. As I did them, I checked off each one. It felt good to see the list dwindle as the week progressed; I knew I was taking better care of myself.

However, I allowed myself leeway so I wouldn't become obsessive about it or anxious if I didn't accomplish the items on the list that week or even the next one. The list thus served as more of a reminder. In time, I learned to do the things within the natural flow of my daily life and no longer in a checklist manner. That way, they were enjoyable and not a chore.

A big factor on my list was doing activities to stay physically fit. I made time to take yoga and karate classes, run, lift weights, coach my children's soccer and basketball teams, and, of course, play tennis. Honoring my body in such ways cleansed my mind of unhelpful chatter. It also resulted in a healthier diet, better sleep, and increased work productivity.

Another important factor was making the time to enjoy my creative currents. Painting and writing books and poetry have been extremely liberating.

Riding the Wave in these ways enables me to care for myself and enjoy a balanced life. It sheds the self-imposed restrictions, judgments, and limitations that in the past led to self-neglect. And importantly, it removes the lingering fear that some unknown adversity might occur if I take the time to care for myself. I now know that I can take care of both myself and other concerns.

Along with learning to take better care of myself, I replaced my special car's engine with a new one. The following year, I reupholstered its leather seats, which had become cracked and discolored.

However, the car still badly needed a new paint job after being on the road for over twenty years, and though I could afford it, for some reason unknown to me, I kept putting it off.

As I was finishing an earlier version of a chapter on self-care for the unpublished book about the Wave I wrote many years ago, I realized how remarkably similar the life of my car and my own life were. When I neglected myself, I neglected my car. When I took better care of myself, I took better care of my car. The car was my alter ego in many ways.

And that's when I also realized how important it was for me to repaint my special car. It was the final touch in restoring it—and, in many ways, myself as well.

Now that we've seen how wave obstructors and enhancers impact riding the Wave, let's next examine the prominent roles they play in determining how we navigate our specific life currents, our life waves, starting with love currents.

INQUIRIES AND REFLECTIONS

- How do you practice self-care?
- What obstacles do you have to overcome to do it?
- Has self-neglect ever caused you emotional or physical pain or harm?
- Do you feel that the need to control impedes the effort?

PART FOUR

Life Waves

CHAPTER EIGHTEEN

Love Flow

Not earlier loves,
Forged by expectant young hearts
And minds more lustful
Than wise.

Where changes came fast,
But few as one.
And where our child's past
Fogged our marital screens.

Not loves where souls still searched,
And hearts still yearned.
Where vulnerable bruises
Went unheeded with loud cries.

No, I speak of a love more wise,
Between two people more whole.
One graced with clear vision
And teachings from mistakes past.

A love that honors thyself,
as much as the union.
That lightens the spirit,
And inspires the mind.

One whose pillars are trust and respect,
And mortar truth and honesty.
And whose greener grass
Lies within its fence.

Yes, I speak of a love
Where souls dance with grace,
And where full hearts and warm bodies
Securely embrace.

This love of which I speak
Is . . . Last Love.
This love of which I speak
Is . . . First Love.

—Daniel A. Miller, "First Love"[1]

LOVE CURRENTS CAN BRING us soulful connection, love, and joy. At their best, they flow both independently and in unison to happy shores and beyond.

Perhaps more so in any other life arena, the interplay of losing control and practicing acceptance is paramount to achieving lasting love and intimacy. Thomas Merton in *No Man Is an Island* expresses their interplay well: "The beginning of this love is the will to let those we love be perfectly themselves, the resolution not to twist them to fit our own image. If in loving them we do not love what they are, but only their potential likeness to ourselves, then we do not love them: we only love the reflection of ourselves we find in them."[2]

Not accepting our partner's ways—annoying and frustrating as they may be—severely dampens the love flow. We are in effect telling them that they aren't good enough as they are. And who wants to feel that way—particularly in matters of the heart?

When we intervene in our loved one's currents—whether through control, judgment, or too-high expectations—we obstruct the love flow. Instead of honoring their personal choices, we pressure them to be other than who they really are and wish to be. To no real surprise, our actions create dissension, resentment, and distrust, thus obstructing the very things needed for intimacy and soulful connection: trust, understanding, and acceptance.

Our love bond is strengthened with greater awareness of what hasn't worked for us in the past. In my earlier love relationships, I was unaware of how controlling I was and its impact on the relationship. Among other intrusions, I pressured my former partners to change their ways, frequently opined what I felt was best for them, and regularly tried to solve their problems.

Although I am much less controlling now, these tendencies persist. Fortunately, my wife calls me out when I overreach. Hence, when I make a know-it-all kind of statement about something she shares, I hear, "How do you know?" My answer is usually a humbling "I don't." And when I impatiently complete her sentences as she is explaining something important to her—a bad habit of mine—she counters, "Will you please stop? That's not at all what I was going to say!" Or if I offer to take over something from her because I question whether she can do it, she looks at me and, in a firm, confident voice asserts, "Danny, I've got this."

A subtler, less apparent—yet equally obtrusive—way in which we intrude on our loved ones' currents is when we are a love enabler. By constantly doing too much for our loved ones, we are effectively trying to control their lives and risk harming them.

The act of enabling isn't defined by any hard and fast rules. We naturally want to give to and do things for those we love and care about. Like many such tendencies, it's a matter of degree and constancy. In general, I ask myself two questions.

The first question is, Are my actions depriving my loved one of being independent and self-reliant? I remember how my favorite uncle would drive my aunt everywhere she wanted or needed to go. As a result, she never learned how to drive since she didn't need to. Remarkably, within several months after my uncle died, my aunt, in her late seventies, learned how to drive and overall became much more independent.

A fine line exists between being loving and compassionate and wanting to do too much for our loved ones. The latter most often takes away rather than gives. My tendency is to want to overhelp with matters my wife may be dealing with. I find that asking "Would you like my help?" makes the line clearer.

The second question I ask myself is, What is the reason or motive behind my action? We can easily discount our true motives for helping our loved ones. More often than I would like to admit, I want to do things for my wife because I believe it would make the situation easier for me.

I used to help her organize her office because I thought it would help her stop putting things in piles. (It didn't.) Truth be told, the main reason—maybe because I am a Virgo!—was that clutter unsettled me a lot. When

I was growing up, my parents always kept our home in perfect order. That was the environment in which I was raised. As I became more aware of that, I leaned into my anxiety around disarray, and it no longer unsettles me as much—and I no longer help my wife with it.

Expecting too much from our loved ones also obstructs the love flow. As mentioned before, high expectations are like a double-edged sword—even sharper in love relationships. We are disappointed when our loved ones don't meet our expectations; in turn, they resent our imposing undue pressure on them.

I need only be reminded of how I react when my wife expects too much from me. I certainly don't feel like giving her a hug or kiss in those moments! Live and let live is a far more congenial approach in love relationships.

On more than a few occasions, when I minded my own business and didn't pressure my wife to change her ways, she later changed them on her own accord. Maybe she wasn't ready or able to make the changes earlier. I suspect, though, that without the pressure from me, she feels freer to examine what is not working for her. Consequently, only by reducing our expectations of our loved ones can trust and intimacy blossom and the love currents flow naturally.

Although we can have compassion for our loved ones and sincerely and lovingly want what's best for them, we cannot truly know what's best for them because we are not them. Most often, we look at things through our own history and filters, not theirs.

Hence, I believe we should accept our loved ones' choices unless we or those we care about are harmed by them. When we don't—whether by pressuring, judging, nagging, or expecting—our love currents won't be in alignment. This isn't always easy. I have to constantly quiet that "I know what's best" part of me and be humble and mindful that my wife's points of view and choices have validity for her. The hard truth is that I am not nearly as omniscient or omnipotent as I am sometimes prone to believe.

Consequently, the love currents flow more expansively when I focus on what I do have control or power over: my role in the relationship. Specifically, my attitudes, actions, reactions, willingness to own up to my own shortcomings and part in relationship dysfunctions, and gratitude for the love and support that my wife gives me.

Below are some intentions that help me do these things:

I will

- Moderate my expectations of my loved one.
- Not pressure her.
- Honor her choices.
- Listen attentively to her concerns.
- Be mindful of her many qualities.
- Be grateful for the many loving things she does for me.

In sum, if I had to say what has been most important in fostering love, intimacy, and deep connection with my wife, it is doing my best to honor and support her personal choices, even though they may be different from what I would have chosen for her or myself.

In doing so, I am blessed to have a loving and soulful connection with my wife for thirty years—one that I could not have imagined possible and one that continues to blossom. Most of the credit for maintaining our strong love bond, however, is due to the kind, caring, and beautiful (in all ways) person that she is.

For parents, the love flow is also impacted by how it aligns with the young and emerging adult waves of their children, as discussed in the next chapter.

INQUIRIES AND REFLECTIONS

- Are you a love controller? In which ways? Do you think your partner would agree?
- Do you listen to the concerns of your loved one without trying to solve them?
- Do you try to see your part (and own up to it) in conflicts with your partner?
- How do you balance wanting to be caring and compassionate toward your loved one and doing too much for them?

CHAPTER NINETEEN

Young Waves

Parents. If you teach us only to be like you, then
how do you expect us to live in the future?

—Lana Miller, sixth-grade graduation speech

OUR CHILDREN HAVE THEIR own waves, with life currents separate and apart from ours. I am a strong believer
that we serve our children best when we don't intrude on
them. As they grow and develop, allowing young people
(age and maturity appropriate) to be the main managers
of their own lives instills in them a sense of independence, responsibility, resilience, and self-esteem that they
likely can't gain in any other way.

An acronym for LOVE sums this idea up well: Let
Others Voluntarily Evolve.

I am not suggesting that we shouldn't provide our
children with support and guidance and share the
wisdom we've gained through our own life experiences.
I'm referring to the propensity to overmanage their
lives—constantly making choices and doing things for
them, feeling we know what's best for them, and pressuring them to do as we say.

But do we really know what's best for our children or
emerging adult children? Are we that omniscient? Much

of the time, I think not. I feel we give insufficient weight to the fact that our children must navigate through vastly different social, cultural, and educational landscapes than we did. All-consuming social media, constantly evolving technology, changing education norms, bullying, and physical danger are just a few of the hurdles our children must traverse.

Our children know these environments much better than we do and must make their decisions and choices within them. Most parents are behind the times. Just remember how we viewed our parents when we were young: we called them "out of touch" and said they were "not with it." Indeed, sometimes I feel I lag at least ten steps behind my children.

That's why I believe that what worked for us may not work for them and that we often don't know what's truly best for them.

Moreover, in not giving due consideration to our children's views, we risk the loss of trust, connection, and contact. Mitchell Rosen, a licensed therapist, expresses the dilemma well. "It's a process of letting go and acceptance. Accepting that my children may know more than me or that their lives truly belong to them requires me to let go. I doubt that I'll ever stop being opinionated but if I don't temper my insistence, I may eat Thanksgiving dinner alone."[1]

Yet as loving, caring parents, it can be extremely difficult to accept our children's ways and choices, especially when their currents appear to be careening toward rocky shores. If you are like me, when your child's heart hurts, your heart hurts. When your child anguishes over something, you anguish over it. (Have you noticed, though, how their hearts and minds almost always heal faster than ours?)

Hence the constant inner struggle. What should we do when our child is hurting from the snide remarks of another child on social media? When his classmates shun him? When she doesn't make the cut for her high school volleyball team? When his teacher continually rides him? And the myriad of other concerns we have about our children's well-being.

Are we enabling when we come to their aid in such situations? Should we let them stumble and experience some hard knocks in the moment, rather than later? Should we lay down the law more than we do? Are we depriving them of valuable learning experiences? Do they really need our protection?

A therapist once suggested that when our children no longer need us, it's usually a sign we've done a good job of raising them. Upon hearing that, I remember feeling both gratified and some remorse. Not feeling needed had a certain emptiness to it.

There are no clear or easy answers to these kinds of questions. Such quandaries underpin what I refer to as the fundamental parental challenge: fulfilling our responsibility as parents to ensure our children's health, safety, and well-being; fostering good morals, values, and ethics; encouraging learning; and ensuring responsible behavior with technology and social media—while not obstructing their personal growth, self-reliance, and life path.

Parents must face this challenge every day—and at times, it feels like every moment. It is always there. And the waters are often murky.

Kahlil Gibran in *The Prophet* offers some wise guidance:

Your children are not your children . . . .

They come through you but not from you,

And though they are with you yet

They belong not to you.

You may give them your love but not your thoughts,

For they have their own thoughts . . . .

Seek not to make them like you.[2]

In terms of the Wave, the challenge can be expressed as follows: At what point are we intervening in or influencing our children's life currents too much and not honoring them enough? And when are we allowing our fears to overpower the trust and faith that our children will reach safe shores on their own?

As you might expect, this is a balancing act in which many factors need to be considered. Pertinent factors include our child's strengths and weaknesses, skills and talents, vulnerabilities, age, and maturity.

We must also determine what's acceptable behavior to us and what's not; what may be harmful to our family or others and what's not; how our personal experiences, biases, and values factor in; and the differences in life circumstances and cultural and societal environments between our childhood and our children's.

What I can share with you are the considerations and practices that have helped me find a better balance for each of my children. The scales were also different for each of them because each of them is different. First and foremost, as mentioned before, I try to act as a loving guide and supporter and, at times, mentor and protector. I try to listen attentively to their issues and concerns regarding school, their peers, work and social involvements, and other matters that concern them. By that, I mean hear them out *without* offering advice or counsel, judging, criticizing, shaming, or admonishing. These obstructors impede open and meaningful discourse.

I have found that most often my children want to vent or express their concerns, not receive advice from me. One parent shared with me, "I let them ask the question before offering advice."

Listening in this manner allows our children to feel safer in confiding in us. It can be a powerful healing tool that promotes trust, respect, and understanding between parents and their children and leads to open and meaningful dialogue on matters in which they don't see eye to eye. Moreover, each is more willing to consider the contrarian views and concerns of the other and more open to changing or modifying their positions. Importantly, this open-minded process can result in agreements and decisions that are more likely to be accepted and adhered to by our children.

I also look at whether my involvement may be obstructing my children's life paths or journeys in some way. I try to view their challenges and struggles as opportunities for them to learn, stretch, become more resilient, and take better care of themselves. I thus consider, Will it deprive her of a valuable learning experience? Make him less independent and resilient? Deny her the sense of accomplishment in doing it herself?

When my children were younger, I considered whether my involvement in their affairs was more to satisfy my ego or concerns—including possible embarrassment or shame—than to serve the higher needs of my children. I queried whether I was overly concerned about how other parents might regard me or my parenting if my children stumbled or fell short.

I am also mindful about whether I am pressuring my children to do what I feel is best for them. When I do, I'm usually met with resistance. This once happened when I urged my eldest daughter to join the well-regarded Toastmasters speaking program after she graduated college to help her overcome her discomfort with public speaking and voicing her views to others. I, too, had been uncomfortable in speaking publicly. I joined Toastmasters while writing *Losing Control, Finding Serenity* in anticipation of speaking opportunities and media appearances following the book's publication. The program's supportive members and varied speaking assignments gave me confidence to speak in front of others.

I thus kept telling my daughter how much Toastmasters would help her at work and socially, encouraging her to join. She kept declining my suggestions until it became a poor subject. Realizing how the subject was impacting our close bond, I stopped bringing it up.

Spring forward nine years: one day, she told me that she had joined Toastmasters and was enjoying and learning a lot from it. A year later, she volunteered to serve as the president of her local chapter. Who would have guessed? As the popular expression goes, "There is a time and place for everything." As a loving father, I could not determine her time and place!

In particular, I am mindful to hold my tongue with respect to my adult children's career choices and paths. On many occasions, I badly wanted to offer my opinions when I witnessed the emotional tolls their jobs were taking on them, or felt their job wasn't a good fit for them or that they should try something different and not put up with this or that.

At the same time, I realized that my advice might quash an opportunity that leads to deeply rewarding career and life experiences. My own winding career path is a testament to how my varied choices, decisions, mistakes, frustrations, and mishaps ultimately brought me unexpected rewards for which I am deeply grateful. I would never have envisioned authoring three personal-growth books in my later years.

That being said, I haven't mastered detaching as much as I would like. There are still times when I become too involved in my children's lives—invariably with unpleasant consequences. A recent example occurred at a family dinner upon seeing how my youngest daughter was disheartened after she received only a minimal pay increase after taking on greater job responsibilities and working more hours.

My other daughter was having an empathetic conversation with her about what was transpiring at her job and asked some pertinent questions. Not agreeing with one of my youngest daughter's responses, I abruptly interrupted their conversation and then proceeded to offer my unsolicited opinion!

There was dead silence at the table. I knew I had quelled an important conversation between the two of them, and the evening ended on a sour note. I apologized to my youngest daughter the next day, but there remained a disconnect between us for several days. I learned another important lesson: mind my own business.

When she called the following week to apprise my wife and me about a difficult conversation she had had with her boss, this time, I patiently listened until she finished relating the conversation and then asked, "Sweetie, are you asking for my input?"

She quickly replied, "Thank you for asking. Not really. I just wanted to express my frustration. I feel much better now."

I also try to be aware of whether my parental fears are dictating my actions. When I have anxiety or feel unsettled concerning my child, I try to take a moment to get in touch with what I am afraid of. Am I fearful she is going around with the wrong friends? Not getting enough sleep or budgeting finances well? Imbibing too much? Once I identify my fears, I lean into and process them and make sure I'm not speculating negatively about future events that haven't yet occurred.

Another factor is not to allow my limited thinking to influence my children's choices. My children generally are more open-minded and more willing than me to pursue new paths and rightfully so—they have more energy and vitality than me.

To be clear, in sharing my parenting beliefs and practices, I am not endorsing permissive parenting where you don't set any rules and boundaries, but rather that parental oversight should be exercised in moderation and be used primarily for our children's health, safety, and moral and spiritual well-being.

The bottom line is this: the degree and extent of a parent's involvement in the affairs of their child is a determination that every parent must make based on the circumstances and the age and nature of their child—and their own propensities. Humility, trust, and acceptance make that choice easier and more closely aligned with our children's currents.

When our parenting days (and worries) pass—to the extent they ever do—our life currents eventually slow and weaken, much like mountain streams do as they arrive at ocean shores. However, as we will see in the next chapter, that doesn't mean we can't still find fulfilling currents to enjoy.

INQUIRIES AND REFLECTIONS

- For the most part, do you allow your children to ride their own waves?

- How do you foster open dialogue with them?

- What factors do you take into account in balancing parental guidance and responsibility with overmanagement of their lives?

- What are your main parental fears? How many are based on your own life experiences? How often do they come to fruition?

CHAPTER TWENTY

Elder Tides

Like as the waves make towards the pebbl'd shore,
So do our minutes hasten to their end

—William Shakespeare

WHEN LATE TIDES ARRIVE, what our currents may lose in strength, endurance, and movement often gain in richness, wisdom, and serenity. My mother, Judy, is a prime example. At the time of this writing, she is ninety-nine years of age and has enjoyed a remarkable late life "spring tide" following the death of my father three years before after seventy-seven years of marriage.

She resides in an assisted-living apartment where she participates in chair exercises and plays bingo almost every day—and is joyous when she wins! She also paints beautiful watercolors of flowers and butterflies in art classes. All this occurred after she endured lengthy COVID-19 pandemic lockdowns in her room with grace and acceptance despite her family not being able to visit her.

Her story supports the findings of research studies about successful aging. The two most formidable obstacles to satisfaction later in life have been found to be loss of control and independence. A study by Deakin University in Australia found that elders' acceptance of what can't be changed in their lives significantly offsets the impact of loss of control and independence.[1]

Acceptance factored in even more than safety, future security, community, personal relationships, and religion. I've noticed that because elders are more accepting in general, they aren't as encumbered by control, judgment, and high expectations. Perhaps that is why elders are more adept at aligning with their life currents than they might have been when they were younger.

I believe another reason may be behind my mother's overall contentment: gratitude. She is appreciative for the loving care that she receives daily at her assisted-living home, where she no longer has to cook meals, do laundry, or take care of her home. In many ways, she is a free bird for the first time in her life.

I, too, try to maintain a deep and daily sense of gratitude for the many blessings in my life—a caring, loving wife, my children navigating their own lives well, good friends, overall good health, and financial security being important ones.

Another blessing of elder tides is the wisdom we gain through our multitude of life experiences, trials and tribulations, and successes and failures. Not only do they make our own lives fuller, but sharing them with others, particularly the young, is a wonderful gift for them and ourselves.

Encouragingly, recent brain cell research and studies have shown that new brain cells can be generated through exercise, social engagement, new activities, and changing daily routines. The process is called *neurogenesis*, where new neurons (brain cells) develop in the hippocampus of the brain, which is responsible for learning information, storing long-term memories, and regulating emotions.

In trying to flow with elder currents myself now, I try to find purpose in my life and feel I can still contribute something of value to others. Writing this book has given me a renewed sense of purpose and the hope that riding the Wave will benefit others as much as it has me. Plus I receive great joy in writing. If nothing else, it has created a lot of new brain cells.

Mentoring others and being of service to friends who have health challenges is also deeply rewarding. And of course I still love playing tennis and painting seascapes and more recently nature-based abstract works. I have discovered that there is a lot of truth in the expression that "age is only a number."

One thing that doesn't appear to wane as we age is our creativity. French impressionist Henri Matisse continued to be highly productive in his final years. Wheelchair bound, he used poles with attached brushes to paint large canvases and created bright assemblages with colored paper cutouts. And remarkably, the renowned abstract expressionist Willem de Kooning continued to paint into his nineties while suffering from Alzheimer's.

The more elders are able to maintain a sense of purpose, meaning, and gratitude in their lives—through whatever activities produce that—the easier it will be for them to accept the losses and limitations that inevitably come with aging.

Whether young or old, we can all have fun riding the creative wave, which the next chapter explores.

INQUIRIES AND REFLECTIONS

- Do you find yourself becoming more accepting of life in general as you get older?
- How difficult is it for you to accept no longer being able to do things you enjoyed when you were younger?
- What do you do to find meaning and purpose in your life?
- Are you less controlling than you were twenty years ago?

CHAPTER TWENTY-ONE

Creative Waves

The creative process is a process of surrender, not control.

—Julia Cameron

CREATIVE BODY-SURFERS ARE ABLE to align with a wave's unpredictable flow in a spontaneous, unforced manner, making the rides more expansive and fun. They hang loose, trust their instincts, and let go.

Our creativity also comes in unpredictable waves. We can't plan, predict, or force it. When we do, we hamstring ourselves. I have learned it's best to stay out of my own way with creative waves, lest disappointment and frustration take over.

As you might surmise, I wrote these last words after becoming frustrated in trying to make a painting that wasn't going anywhere into one that was—and failing miserably.

I had been pleased by how unexpectedly well my previous painting had turned out. I quickly began another one full of expectations—the death knell for any artist. I found myself hoping and waiting for some wonderful "accident" to occur that would suddenly improve it. And of course it didn't happen.

An instructor in a plein air painting workshop I once attended said, "If I'm lucky, one out of seven paintings turn out well." That was coming from a highly skilled artist. So why should I expect better odds? Why do I so often think that my paintings are going to turn out well? Supreme optimism? I don't think so. Masterful technique? Who am I kidding! Am I being unmindful of the very nature and mystery of the creative process? That's more like it.

Simply put, our creative currents don't flow on demand.

We can't will or wish them to appear. But we can create more space for them to appear by being mindful of the wave obstructors that easily intrude upon our creative currents. High expectations, limited thinking, and impatience make us press on when a work is not ready to be completed, overthink when things should be kept simple, play it safe when we should take creative risks, and fret when we should just trust the process.

Judgment and the inner critic prompt us to focus on what's wrong about a work instead of what may be right about it, causing us to become creatively hamstrung. All such forms of control inhibit the creative process—whether in art, writing, music, dance, song, or other performance— by restricting freedom of thought, of process, of motion, and ultimately of connection with our soul center.

Lord Thomas Babington Macaulay expressed it well: "It seems that the creative faculty and the critical faculty cannot exist together in their highest perfection."[1]

To keep these two faculties separate, I try to moderate my expectations. Maintaining realistic expectations is especially difficult when I begin a work on a high note.

Hopes and expectations for a masterly finish invariably submerge my creative currents.

I thus try to be grateful for good beginnings and not discouraged by poor ones and trust whatever later unfolds. It may turn into an unexpected gift. I once decided to begin a painting with no expectations and just enjoy the physicality of mixing the colors and applying the paint to the canvas in multiple ways with a palette knife and a variety of brush types.

To avoid focusing on how the painting looked, I turned the canvas upside down and sideways several times and continued painting. I became enthralled in the process of freely applying paint. In fact, I didn't even realize that the painting was finished until I turned the canvas around the final time and saw a beautiful (to me) abstract painting. (A photo of the painting, titled *Free Flow*, can be viewed at danielamiller.com/paintings.)

I have no idea how it all came together other than I just enjoyed the process and suspended judgment. For a representational or figurative painter like me, it felt like a miracle. Excited, I tried doing another abstract piece right away. That was the problem: I *tried*! I'll let you guess how that one turned out.

I also try not to stay too long with a work, whether a painting, a poem, or my writing. On too many occasions, I overthought and overworked a piece, losing the freshness and vitality of my initial vision. The metaphor that comes to mind is how when you overcook pasta, it becomes soft and mushy.

Fortunately, I didn't stay too long with the painting of waves, a cropped portion of which appears on the cover of this book. (The full version is on my website.) After watching an online tutorial by artist Andrew Tischler[2] on how to paint waves, I decided to get my feet wet by practicing on a small, inexpensive canvas board.

With no expectations and feeling relaxed and free, in less than two hours, I had a nice seascape gracing my canvas. When I looked at the painting the next morning, I asked myself, "Is it done? Should I stop?" Mindful of my propensity, I answered yes and yes.

Although not always successful, I also try to keep it simple. Less is invariably more. Thus, when I sense I may be starting to overwork a piece, I take a break, perhaps stretching, taking a walk, or just going outdoors and breathing some fresh air. Or I just stop painting for the day.

Sometimes I will put a painting aside for weeks or months—even for over a year. When I return to it, I bring a fresh eye and renewed interest. Almost always, I see aspects I hadn't noticed before, such as compositional or value deficiencies. I also notice interesting facets that warrant exploring. In fact, I might discard my original vision or intention for a work as I pursue an entirely different path.

I do the same with my writing. After I completed the first draft of this book, I took a writing vacation for several months. When I reread the manuscript, I noticed quite a few grammar and syntax errors and content that was redundant and not pertinent. I felt like I was my own editor. I took several more writing breaks before finalizing the manuscript.

I also go back and forth between painting and writing—sometimes within the same hour (as I have done in writing portions of this chapter). I find that one creative endeavor enhances the other, bringing freshness to both works. I think of this as creative cross-pollination. I don't think I'm alone in this. In my mind's eye, I can visualize Tony Bennett and Joni Mitchell, excellent vocalists and artists, singing as they paint!

I also view my paintings from different positions and angles. I've even observed them through a mirror. By varying the perspective in such ways, I see details with a different eye, spotting distractions but also interesting highlights I hadn't noticed before.

Sometimes unwanted feelings arise as I'm writing or painting—anxiety, frustration, and impatience among them. When I don't address these feelings, they take the spontaneity and joy out of the creative experience, and the work usually suffers. When this occurs, I try to lean into and process the unsettling feelings, as explained in chapter 15.

We all have unique creative currents that encompass our aesthetics, styles, skills, vulnerabilities, and core beliefs and values. We need to honor, trust, and remain true to them. They are a vital part of who we are. We don't need to please anyone but ourselves.

Ultimately, the creative process is enhanced by embracing its ebbs and flows, letting go, trusting, accepting, and not judging. At its best, the creative act becomes highly enriching—even spiritual—as freedom and openness of ideas and process gel seamlessly with technique to produce works of beauty and meaning. At such moments, I truly feel at one with my soul center, and for me, there is no better feeling.

Another highly enjoyable wave is hindered by many of the same obstructions as creative waves. The next chapter looks at this very active wave.

INQUIRIES AND REFLECTIONS

- Do you think of yourself as a creative being? If not, why?

- In which ways do you express your creative nature? How important a role does it play in your life?

- How do you avoid forcing your creative endeavors?

- Do you think perfectionism and creativity can ever be complementary? What about judgment and creativity?

CHAPTER TWENTY-TWO

Sports Waves

It's just about being in the zone, in any sport, be it
football, basketball or baseball.

—Mark Teixeira

SPORTS WAVES ARE SOME of the most exciting and exhilarating waves to ride. When we are in the zone, the game
or match flows almost seamlessly and effortlessly. As our
confidence builds, the breaks just seem to come our way.
Yet aligning with the flow and rhythm of the game is very
challenging for most athletes mainly because of how control and high expectations obstruct the currents.

Competitive sports are a hotbed for control. The
intensity and pressure of competition propels athletes
to constantly press or force the action even when it goes
against the flow of the game, causing them to tighten up,
make poor decisions, and in general not play within their
skill set.

Because of my control-based mindset, I haven't
aligned with the tennis currents nearly as much as I
would like. When I try to hit the ball too hard, I lose my
rhythm and make more unforced errors; if I swing too
softly, the balls usually go in the net. And when I think

about too many fundamentals of the game while playing, I end up doing none of them well.

No sport is immune from the impact of controlling actions. When golfers try to hit the ball far by swinging too hard off the tee, they often look up and shank the ball. When quarterbacks force passes against tight coverage, they are prone to more interceptions. And when running backs strive too hard for extra yardage, they risk fumbling the ball.

Overanalysis is another impediment to aligning with the sports currents. In baseball, batting slumps are prolonged when players try too hard to come out of them. They take extra batting practice to little avail. Some players analyze their swing in detail with the help of film and batting coaches, trying to spot defects and propose adjustments, only to become more mired in their slumps. The irony is that when the players finally stop trying so hard, they usually begin hitting or pitching the ball better.

When former Atlanta Braves pitching ace John Smoltz was mired in a 2–11 record at the All-Star break, he said over analyzing every bad pitch he made only made matters worse. When he stopped obsessing about his pitches, he was 12–2 for the remainder of the season.

Paradoxically, the more athletes try to overperform, the more they usually underperform, as future Hall of Famer Albert Pujols can attest to. After signing a ten-year $240 million contract with the California Angels, he started the season in a huge batting slump, hitting only .194 with no home runs in the first month. His performance improved remarkably during the following three months, as he batted .303 with twenty-four home runs.

When asked what accounted for his sudden improvement, Pujols replied, "I think everyone was pressing, not just myself, but I was the face because I signed the big contract, and I had to show people I was worth every penny. . . . When I decided not to try to do too much, that's when things started to turn."[1]

Similarly, in explaining why he had an off season after signing a large contract, former Los Angeles Dodger Adrian Gonzalez said he was "trying too hard. . . . This game is not one in which you make things happen. You have to let things happen."[2]

I have observed and personally experienced certain mindsets and practices that help athletes optimize their skills within the flow of the game. One is to stay within your game. When playing against a strong player or team, we naturally try to compensate by doing too much or changing the way we play. Invariably, this compels us to play outside our comfort zones and skill sets.

Professional boxers learn the painful consequences when they don't stay within their game or skill set. In championship fights, when boxers known for their great footwork and defensive skills try to slug it out with heavy hitting punchers, they usually wind up on the deck.

When my doubles partner is having an off day, my inclination used to be to serve harder than normal, try to cover too much court, and go after balls that were beyond my reach. The results were that I tired myself out and made more unforced errors. Now I focus on staying within my own game so that it, too, doesn't falter, and remember that I am powerless over how my partner performs.

We also need to adjust to the flow of the game. As with all life waves, sports waves have their unpredictable ebbs and flows. The action is constantly shifting, and momentum can change in a second. Top athletes adjust to the flow and rhythm of the game, looking for opportunities to apply their skills more impactfully.

Chris Paul and LeBron James, two perennial basketball all-stars, are particularly adept at sensing the flow of the game and identifying how they can apply their skill sets in ways most favorable to their teams. Paul meshes his ball handling, ball distribution, and shooting skills almost seamlessly. He plays differently from game to game and even within the same game, selecting his moments to maximize his and his teammates' performance. Sometimes he is the aggressive scorer and at other times, he is the needed facilitator.

James, too, is adept at sizing up how a game is going and what his team needs of his broad skill set. Depending on the situation or point in the game, he might shoot three pointers, drive aggressively to the hoop drawing fouls, generate scoring opportunities for his teammates, or provide a combination of these skills.

I have also learned the importance of maintaining realistic expectations of what I can accomplish. Much like with creative endeavors, overly high expectations of my performance raise the stakes and increase the pressure to try too hard or do more than I should.

When I am not playing well, I moderate my expectations, don't judge myself, and save my analysis for after the match. I've had my share of bad days on the court. I used to worry about them and give them too much importance. I now keep in mind that I've had many good days following bad ones. I now consider them off days, not bad ones. Sometimes our bodies simply don't do what we want them to or we may not have slept well or might have other things on our mind.

It also helps to visualize performing well. Before a match, I close my eyes and visualize getting in touch with a smooth rhythm. I picture myself moving and swinging my racket in an easy, confident manner. I try to be specific: seeing the ball roll off my fingertips when I toss it up to serve, timely drawing back the racket for a forehand, and staying light on my feet. I even visualize playing actual points.

For me, though, the most important mindset is to trust my game, which is to say trust myself and my body. I constantly practice improving my skills, but when the match starts, I trust that what I've honed in practice will flow over to the game and that my body will instinctively know what to do. That's not the time to get mental; it would only impede the flow. On the court, my mantra now is simple: "Trust, and have fun!"

We run into another kind of highly competitive wave—one that is quite often accompanied by stress, anxiety, and sometimes loss of sleep when we don't align with it: the work wave.

INQUIRIES AND REFLECTIONS

- How do you get in the flow and rhythm of the game?

- Do you strive for perfection in your athletic endeavors? What are the results? Are you able to moderate your expectations?

- How do you balance the mental and physical aspects of your game? Which do you find more important?

- As an exercise, the next time you're playing your favorite sport, don't think about anything except trusting your game.

CHAPTER TWENTY-THREE

Work Waves

Some of us think holding on makes us strong, but
sometimes it is letting go.

—Hermann Hesse

WHEN I RETURNED TO work following my facial surgeries, I noticed something remarkable. My business had
been functioning quite well without all my constant
direction. A few projects even had positive outcomes with
little input from me. This was a quite a revelation. Could
it be that I couldn't influence the outcome of events as
much as I thought? Were some matters best left alone or
to proceed at their own pace?

I was certainly curious to find out. I began observing
the ebb and flow of work life. I noticed that like real waves,
each project or transaction had its own unique course
and pace. Sometimes a transaction would flow smoothly;
at other times, it would halt abruptly. And like murky
waters, some matters were unclear or uncertain without
any apparent direction. Quite often, a stop-and-go pattern
developed—the to and fro of the Wave. I discovered that
as long as I was observant and patient and didn't force
things, productive paths and opportunities usually arose.

I thus began participating in the ever-evolving workflow in a more nonintrusive manner. I didn't press or resist as much as I had in the past, nor was I quick to judge or assume that my way was the best or only way. I began trusting my instincts and intuition more, waiting for opportune times in which to apply my skill and experience.

My involvement was often minimal. Sometimes only a suggestion at the appropriate moment would be enough. Other times, I'd do nothing if I wasn't sure what to do. I also listened more to my staff and welcomed their input. When I overreached, which I did a lot in the beginning, I usually knew because the workflow would be disrupted. I would then tread water and wait for more opportune currents to evolve.

The results of doing business in this way were remarkable. I avoided costly diversions of time and resources. My pervasive sense of urgency lessened and I was considerably more relaxed. In fact, work became enjoyable for the first time. And importantly, I made better decisions.

In short, losing work control has been transformative for me in navigating the work currents. It allows me to step back and see the bigger picture. In my real estate business, I am more able than ever before to devote my time and energy to what is truly relevant and spot important trends and trouble areas and adapt accordingly.

That's not to say that losing work control is easy. It's a daily challenge for me. The workplace is rife with control practices. I don't think it's an overstatement to say that the workplace is one of the most prominent arenas in which humanity's primal drive for sustenance is played out. Some graciously refer to it as just "trying to get ahead" or "making ends meet," but in truth, it can be argued that much of workplace behavior is nothing less than the survival of the fittest. In certain ways, the scavenger and plunderer of primitive times has evolved into the breadwinner of today.

Thus, business owners must constantly be vigilant, for who knows what dangers lurk in the waters— ambitious new competitors, untrustworthy workers, scammers, whistleblowers, and thieves of trade secrets. Conversely, workers fear demotions, loss of benefits, and not keeping up with ever-increasing learning curves. And both employers and workers fear that the other may not respond reasonably if their issues and concerns are addressed forthrightly. Hence, we often find workers quitting without adequate notice and employers dismissing or demoting employees with little or no warning.

To be sure, control has its place. Efficient practices and policies, quality control procedures, proper supervision, and adequate safety and security all need to be established and maintained. However, we also need to distinguish between such organizational best practices and domineering impulses. The latter are primarily triggered by our fears, expectations, anger, frustration, and greed. These control catalysts make us prone to acting impulsively, confrontationally, and contrary to our best interests. As such, we become out of sync with the work currents.

To avoid such obstructions, as previously mentioned, I try to lean into these unwanted feelings and address their underlying causes and avoid speculating about events that may never come to pass. That provides me with a truer perception about what is actually at stake, and I can better see the realistic choices and options that may have been obscured from me before.

A case in point was when following the vandalism at one of our industrial tenant's premises, an attorney sent us a letter that included false factual assertions and demanded that we install a security gate at the entrance to the property and security cameras around the property and provide a night security guard. The tenant threatened to stop paying rent until we met their demands.

I was angered by the harsh tone of the letter and the nature of the demands. However, rather than respond quickly in kind, I took some time to gather all the facts, consider security options, review our lease agreement, and process my anger. In doing so, I realized that the tenant's actions were likely based on fear of recurring vandalism and the resulting financial losses.

We determined that a security entrance gate was unfeasible—even if we agreed to install one—since it would prevent ingress and egress to the property by some of our other tenants. We then informed the tenant that our lease agreement specifically stated that the landlord had "no obligation whatsoever" to provide security or a guard service for the tenant and that the tenant assumed "all responsibility for the protection" of the premises. We said that we would install additional lighting adjacent to the premises, but the tenant would need to pay the rent if they wished to avoid an eviction action. We received the tenant's rent several days later.

I also try to assess what's really at stake in matters that concern or worry me. They often are not that important in the overall scheme of things. Not everything is a crisis, but almost anything can become one if we don't take the time to consider what's at stake. Simple questions such as "How important is it?" and "Does it have to be done now?" and "Are other options available?" provide better perspective. Many times, I conclude that the wisest choice is to do nothing.

Importantly, working in a truthful, trusting, and accepting manner enables us to align better with the work currents. Truth and candor in business are powerful deterrents to animus and dissension while instilling trust, cooperation, and open discourse. When we are not truthful in our work and business dealings, we are attempting to manipulate people and events, thereby obstructing the natural work rhythm. In my own business dealings, I can't think of a time or occasion in which being truthful or owning up to my mistake worked to my disadvantage.

Accepting the things in work or business that we are powerless to change allows us to focus on what we can change or improve, resulting in increased efficiency and productivity. If I'm not sure whether I can influence events, I can try and see what happens. If I'm met with noticeable resistance or conflict or a sense that matters are going awry, I can back off and move on to matters where I can have some impact.

Trusting that we will be okay—or can find a way—regardless of work setbacks, adversities, or unexpected occurrences lessens fear and anxiety and the need to control. A good friend jokingly said that during hard economic times such as the Great Recession of 2008, "I've been going bankrupt for thirty years!" Like my friend, I am mindful that I've overcome many business struggles and crises in the past, and I'm still here and very likely will be tomorrow as well!

While the life waves we've thus far looked at all have their crests and troughs—and at times ripples and rip tides—much of the time we can find ways to remain in safe harbors when encountering truly challenging currents. Some waves, however, are so powerful, unmanageable, and out of control that our well-being is at risk when encountering or engaging them. Part 5 examines some of these troubled waters.

INQUIRIES AND REFLECTIONS

- Are you apprehensive about relinquishing control at work? Why or why not?

- Do you often have a sense of urgency at work? Do you ever consider whether it is truly urgent?

- Do you find yourself engaged in limited thinking or resisting change at work?

- As an exercise, when dealing with important work matters, consider saying to yourself, "I trust that everything will work out."

PART FIVE

Troubled Waters

CHAPTER TWENTY-FOUR

Addictive Waves

We admitted we were powerless over alcohol—
that our lives had become unmanageable.

—1st step, Alcoholics Anonymous

TWO OF MY HIGH school friends were so hooked on surfing that almost every Friday or Saturday they would rise early and drive seventy miles to the beaches of Orange County. They sometimes missed classes and were so tired when they returned, they had little time and energy to study, and their grades faltered. Although surfing was a healthy passion in many ways, their being addicted to it carried adverse consequences well beyond high school.

Waves of addiction are cunning, baffling, and powerful, and they are more prevalent than ever in no small part due to the opioid crisis and the COVID-19 pandemic. The lives of most addicts reel out of control, leading to a life of dependency, pain, and suffering for themselves and those who care about them.

In short, addicts are totally out of alignment with their life currents.

Children's debilitating drug and alcohol addictions are particularly sad and challenging for parents. Some of my friends have suffered unabatedly in trying to cope with their children's addictions. Household theft, deceit, manipulation, and even violence are not uncommon.

Parental fears run rampant, justifiably so. It is extremely difficult for them not to intervene in attempts to slow their children's escalading currents. Many parents will do most anything to keep their children off the streets and out of jail, often to no avail.

A sad consequence is that these parents' own lives often spin out of control and become unmanageable, engulfing them and their families in constant riptides and undertows. Some have found relief—and even serenity—accepting they are powerless over their children's addictions. They are no less fearful or loving of their children but have concluded that their lives—and hopefully their children's—will have a greater chance of recovery if they allow them to suffer the consequences of their actions instead of trying to continually rescue them.

My friend Mike is one of these parents. His youngest son, Justin, had been addicted to drugs and alcohol since his early teens. In the beginning, Mike and his wife, Alison, constantly tried to help Justin overcome his addiction and stay out of trouble by enforcing strict discipline at home, hovering over him much of the time and pleading and trying to reason with him.

Nothing worked. Justin's addictions went unabated. He was in and out of rehab centers on multiple occasions before he turned twenty-one, and nothing changed. After he came of age, he was in rehab three more times before turning thirty, also without improvement—each time with his parents footing the bill.

What did change was that Mike's and Alison's lives spun more and more out of control. Mike recounted, "It got so crazy that one time I chased my son down the street at four a.m. in the morning in my underwear, screaming at him to get back in the house."

When I saw Mike at a men's recovery workshop some months later, I couldn't help but notice his bright face and smile and wonderful sense of humor. When I asked him what had changed, he explained:

"I finally realized—and accepted—that there was absolutely nothing I could do to control or cure my son's addictions. I knew it was simply beyond my power to do and, importantly, that my wife and I weren't responsible for where he is at today in his life. The reality is that he is a very sick person suffering from a very debilitating disease. All my efforts to help him were fruitless and likely made matters worse for him.

"I do call Justin daily to let him know how much I love and care for him. But I also accept his addiction for what it is—a pernicious disease that only he has the power to overcome, God willing. As a result, a tremendous burden and a lot of stress has been lifted from our shoulders."

As was the case with my wife's alcohol addiction, Mike's story illustrates that acceptance does not mean condoning another's poor behavior or choices but rather accepting the underlying reality of a situation without judgment and understanding that we are powerless over changing another's self-destructive ways. Doing so lessens the shame, guilt, and unrelenting burden, bringing us greater serenity. In short, it allows us to navigate our own life currents better.

While alcohol and drugs are the most prominent addictive waves, there are also other powerful ones

—tobacco, food, sex, gambling, and now video games and social media among them—all of which cause riptides for the users and those who love and care about them.

Control plays a prominent role in most addictions. Addicts feel ashamed and powerless over their inability to control their addictions, although many don't admit it. To counter their anxiety and try to gain some semblance of control over their imploding currents, they feel compelled to hold on tightly in search of stability. They mainly do this by trying to exert external control over aspects of their (and others') lives that they believe are creating their anxiety and helplessness. This attempt often comes in the form of deceiving, blaming, and mistreating their friends and loved ones and manipulating people in general. Threats, accusations, rages, fabrications, and repeated promises abound.

However, just as with trying to control other areas of their lives, the tighter addicts hold on and try to control their addictive currents, the more out of control their lives become. Hope for recovery lies in their admitting that they are powerless over their addictions and that their lives have become unmanageable.

As such, they must let go of any denial they harbor. Overcoming denial is usually a gradual process, peeled off in layers, until finally the painful consequences of their continuing to use become greater than the pain of not using. At that point, some addicts become willing to seek recovery. Hence, people often say addicts must first hit bottom before the light of awareness shines on their denials.

Unfortunately, admission alone may not be enough for recovery from the powerful waves of addiction. An addict's courage and willingness to change his or her self-destructive ways are also needed. This is a formidable obstacle that many addicts are unable to meet alone, if at all.

Many have found recovery through participation in twelve-step programs, Alcoholics Anonymous being the most prominent, where with the support and encouragement of fellow members, they learn by admitting the unmanageability of their lives and surrendering to a "Higher Power" (or God of their understanding), they can begin their journey of repair and recovery and gain some serenity in their lives.

Friends and families of addicts have similarly found help in the Al-Anon twelve-step program, where they learn the foolhardiness of trying to control or solve the addictions of their loved ones. Instead, they learn to detach from the forceful spirals of addictive currents and focus on making their own lives better, as my friend Mike and I did. Hence, instead of making waves, members learn there is a greater chance for recovery—both for the addicts and themselves—if they allow addictive currents to weaken by themselves.

Addicts are not the only combative people we have to deal with in our lives. The next chapter looks at some others that can easily disrupt our life currents.

INQUIRIES AND REFLECTIONS

- Do you try to help friends or family members who suffer from addictions? In which ways? Are they effective?

- Are you able to set limits, including financial, on what you are willing to do for an addict?

- How is your life impacted by trying to avert an addict's destructive ways?

- Are you able to be more compassionate toward addicts by viewing their addictions as diseases or sicknesses over which they have no real control?

CHAPTER TWENTY-FIVE

Combative Waves

A smooth sea never made a skilled sailor.

—Anonymous

JUST AS BODY-SURFERS MUST protect themselves from thrashing rogue waves, we must do the same when encountering combative, divisive people in our lives—to wit, the waves of control freaks, vengeful litigants, intrusive neighbors, hostile workers, and antagonistic people in general, all of whom we fear might cause us harm.

When we clash with such people, the riptides and undertows can be severe. In the years since the battle with my former business partner, I have worked hard to stay clear of such troubled waters. I no longer quickly draw swords; when I do, I know I will mainly cut myself.

Instead, I try to accept my foes as they are. That may seem counterintuitive. You may wonder why I would want to accept people who look to cause me trouble or harm. Wouldn't they be the last people I would want to accept? I fully understand those sentiments; for years, I felt the same way. It's clearly unnerving to think about accepting the people that cause us great grief and even more challenging to do so.

The simple answer though is that it allows me to navigate wiser currents. When I look back, I realize that I suffered unnecessarily from my refusal to accept such people as they were, both in terms of greater anguish and my ill-conceived responses to their words and actions.

This was particularly true in the case of my former business partner, who I felt had betrayed me in my time of need. My refusal and inability to accept this person for who he was—a manipulative, scheming businessman with few scruples—and then act in my own best interests instead of a retaliatory manner contributed to my serious health problems and resulted in my near bankruptcy.

Importantly, accepting combative people as they are doesn't mean that we condone or excuse what they are doing or have done. Nor does it mean we shouldn't take action to protect ourselves. We should. Rather, it means that we accept we are powerless over changing their ways and we are better served by acting or making decisions aligned with that reality.

Thus, when encountering combative people, I try not to act or react impulsively. That gives me time to assess what's actually at stake with the grievance and its over-all importance. In doing so, I ask myself the following questions:

- "Is what they are doing truly that harmful?"
- "Am I taking the matter too personally?"
- "Am I making a mountain out of a molehill?"
- "Am I speculating too much about what might happen?"
- "Do I know all the facts?"
- "Am I misconstruing things?"

I also don't assume the person is out to do me harm. Viewing the situation from my adversary's perspective or looking through their lenses softens the sharp edge of my anger and resentment. Like my own, people's behavior is often based on their fears, anxieties, insecurities, and self-interests and not on any intent to do harm. Understanding that allows me not to take matters so personally and emotionally detach from their conduct, as I did with the tenant who threatened to stop paying rent if we didn't meet his security demands.

I earlier failed to do that with a commercial tenant who, during the COVID-19 pandemic, was taking advantage of the rent moratorium by remaining in his space and living there after his lease had expired and not paying rent for over a year. He kept making false accusations and coming down with different mutations of the coronavirus.

Angered by the deceptions and taking the matter very personally, we filed an eviction suit for possession of the space, but we did not seek any past due rent. To my chagrin, we lost. The judge ruled that even though the tenant's lease had expired, he could remain in possession for as long as the moratorium remained in effect.

The way I was able to later release the feeling that I was wronged was to view the situation from the tenant's perspective. He was elderly and financially stressed, looked to be in poor health, and had nowhere else to live. I was thus able to see that he was not intentionally trying to harm me, but simply trying to stay alive with a roof over his head.[1]

I further consider whether I can realistically change the person or situation. Most of the time, I can't. Even if I feel I can have some impact on the matter or person, I consider whether any success is worth the cost in terms of energy, anguish, and loss of sleep. In my experience, most often, it's not.

More recently, this helped me in dealing with a situation where another business partner was not distributing my share of the income from a joint real estate investment in which I had a minority interest and no say in operations. When I inquired about why he was not making the distributions, he kept giving me different reasons for the delay. I believed (but wasn't sure) that his motive was to pressure me to sell my interest to him at a low price. There may have been other reasons unbeknownst to me. I also knew that needless speculation would only upset me more.

Unlike in the past, I took time to consider my options. Should I just keep inquiring each month as to why he was not making the distributions? Should I put my partner on formal legal notice that he was violating the terms of our ownership agreement? Or should I simply do nothing and patiently wait and see?

I chose the latter rather than risk unnecessary acrimony—the opposite of what I had done several decades earlier with my former partner. Several months later, without explanation, I received a check in the mail for considerably more than I had anticipated and have received regular distributions since.

In telling that story, I'm not suggesting that we should be meek or passive in dealing with divisive or combative people. At times, assertive action is needed. It's more a matter of knowing what we can and can't control, accepting we are powerless over changing others in any meaningful way, and recognizing where our true power lies in any given situation.

Still, knowing how hard it can be not to take things personally when dealing with combative people, I consider whether I had some part in the grievance. Owning up to my own role is tough because the initial sting makes it easy to dismiss what I may have contributed to the grievance. It takes self-honesty and abeyance of my ego to admit that I may be at least partly at fault.

However, with few exceptions, I have learned that no matter how innocent or right I thought I was about someone's disturbing or disruptive acts, I was in some way partly responsible for them. I may have been smug, dismissive, neglectful, or curt. Or I may have misconstrued what the person said or did or hadn't taken the time to ascertain all the facts. When I am able to see my part in what has transpired, it takes the emotional edge off things, and I can respond in a more composed manner.

Finally, to avoid overreacting to combative people, I try to process my fears. Fear of what a foe might do makes us reactive instead of realistically assessing how we can best secure our borders.

The next chapter examines one combative wave that is so threatening and powerful it impacts everyone's life currents. It is the most prevalent tidal wave of our times: the Great Divide.

INQUIRIES AND REFLECTIONS

- Are you able to accept combative people as they are?

- Do you automatically assume a combative person intends to harm you in some way? Do you ever consider what other motives they might have?

- How much does fear or anger influence your interactions with divisive people? Have such emotions ever caused you to act in ways that were detrimental to your interests?

- Do you ever consider whether you had some role or part in a grievance? How long does it take to acknowledge it?

CHAPTER TWENTY-SIX

Today's Tidal Wave

Vacuum of the unknown,
Uneven compass
From Entrance to Exit, and
Thought to action.

Abode to worry and anxiety,
Suffering abyss when our
Wants aren't of this Moment,
And our fears can't find their courage.

A translucent Shrine,
Sensed vaguely as
The Space Between
And seen only as
"   "

Yet in its Halls
Expectations cease,
Interests align,
Denial discovers Awareness,
Resistance shrinks to Acceptance, and
Our quest for Serenity eases as
Real Truth Reveals.

—Daniel A. Miller, "The Space Between"

I THINK FEW WOULD argue that our country is more deeply divided now than any time since the Civil War. Disparagement, derision, and outright hostility rule the Great Divide that exists within today's social, cultural, and political currents.

The tidal wave encompassing such divisive issues as climate change, abortion, racial and gender equality, gun control, voting rights, free speech, and immigration impact all our life currents. We live in so-called alternate universes—each having vastly different core beliefs, values, and skepticism of intentions, facts, and realities. This is not surprising given the vast number of information channels—cable news, print media, the internet, social media, podcasts, science and cultural institutions, and government agencies, to name just a few.

In the past, I felt uncomfortable or unqualified entering these turbulent waters. However, given the ever-increasing abrasive discord we face today, I feel compelled to try to lessen the acrimony and foster understanding and unity in some way, not only for myself but also for my children's and grandchildren's sakes.

But where and how does one begin to help heal or bridge the Great Divide? Is it even possible or worth the effort? The more salient question, though, is this: Do we dare risk the consequences of doing nothing?

Not me—not any longer.

When I ponder these questions and the formidable obstacles, the wise counsel of the Chinese philosopher Lao-tzu in the Tao Te Ching comes to mind: "The journey of a thousand miles begins with a single step."

Should we not try taking some single steps, even if we don't agree what those steps are or know if they will make a difference? Again, my answer is yes because we can't afford not to. This writing, then, is one single step I am taking. Perhaps we can journey together.

Acceptance Heals and Unifies

I strongly believe our best hope in lessening the Divide is through acceptance of the other side, particularly people we strongly disagree with, dislike, or maybe even detest. I believe acceptance is the best way in which today's alternate universes can begin communicating with one another.

Three major gifts of acceptance—trust, connection, and understanding—can be brought about through acceptance conversations. These can help us to discover common ground and interests, foster clearer understanding, and create paths for healing and repair. Acceptance conversations take into account how the wave obstructors we've explored in the book—particularly judgment, expectations, limited thinking, arrogance, fear, and anger—widen the Divide. They also demonstrate how the wave enhancers—acceptance, trust, truth, and humility—narrow it.

The conversations can be structured or informal, virtual or in person. They can be on a one-on-one basis or in groups with people who have diverse social, cultural, and political views. They can be with family members whose extreme views have shredded apart entire kinship groups as well as with longtime friends whose relationships have frayed over the years. They can take place at work, school, church, or community gatherings and organizations.

We need to make an effort to engage in such conversations with an open mind and without harsh judgment or contempt. Dr. Martin Luther King Jr. touched upon the importance of doing so when he said, "You have very little morally persuasive power with people who can feel your underlying contempt of them." From such a nonabrasive, nonconfrontational mindset, the opportunity exists for a shift in focus from trying to demean, change, or convince others to finding common ground and interests that can lead to improving all our lives and the world.

Whatever setting or format is chosen for these conversations, the following interrelated mindsets and practices are catalysts for more meaningful dialogue:

Seek and explore shared interests—Instead of focusing on your differences and what divides you, seek and talk about shared interests and values. Subjects might include the desire to be a caring, loving parent and taking pride in your children; the challenges in caring for your elders; talking about where you grew up; discussing your favorite foods, hobbies, and pastimes; and conversing about your favorite sports teams, athletes, and entertainers.

Exploring such common interests lays a positive framework for the discussion of deeper matters—in the moment or later—by creating a human connection and providing a fuller picture of the other person as well as where they are coming from on divisive issues—in short, seeing the humanity in the other. Thus, in group settings, participants should be encouraged to take a few minutes to introduce themselves, sharing what they do, what brings them to the conversation, and what their interests, concerns, and hopes are.

Be civil—You'll have a greater chance that people will understand or consider contrarian views when they are presented in a thoughtful, respectful manner and without an attitude that we know what's right or best. It is a discussion, not an argument or debate. People will most always be dismissive or resistant if you are rude, harsh, or contemptuous. Hence, don't raise your voice, lecture, dismiss, or demean.

Be willing to listen and hear others out—Make an effort to listen attentively to what people have to say without interruption and with as little judgment, or criticism as possible. Avoid formulating responses or rebuttals as others are speaking, which will only impede clear understanding about what is being shared.

This clearly is not easy, for we naturally want to judge others. The stronger our own views, the greater our propensity is to judge others' views. It will help if you are genuinely interested and curious. Ask questions or seek clarification when needed to better understand positions and avoid misinterpretations. Real listening can be very healing. It makes us feel good when we are seen and heard, and we will likely be more open to reciprocating in kind.

Be mindful that the main purpose of acceptance conversations is to establish trust, connection, and common ground, not to convince or convert, which will likely have the opposite effect. None of this is to say that we should discard our own beliefs and values or not express or defend them. It behooves us to do so with civility and humility, lest we risk making existing wedges wider and deeper.

Don't assume others are out to harm you—While others' views may be extreme or repugnant to you, that doesn't necessarily mean others are out to do you harm. As mentioned before, people often act based on their deeply held beliefs, values, and self-interests—just as we do ourselves. Understanding that, try not to take what is said personally or be combative in addressing divisive issues. Responding in a clear, calm manner will be more productive.

Be truthful—In supporting our views or countering others', we can easily stretch the truth or assert facts whose veracity is not documented or vetted to prove our point. Remember, we are not trying to win an argument. We are seeking mutual understanding and trust. Acknowledging our lack of knowledge or uncertainty about a matter or an issue or simply saying, "I don't know" or "You may be right" makes us appear more human and sincere, and our commentary will likely be better received.

Be humble—Don't be smug, arrogant, or righteous. Many people, myself included, are prone to believing that they know what's best or what's right for others—and too often expound on it! Such know-it-all-ness creates strong barriers to constructive dialogue. What's right or good for ourselves may not be so for others.

Understand and address people's fears and concerns— Many beliefs and views are based on fear or past events and heighten defiance to considering contrary viewpoints. Remember, in many cases, FEAR often stands for false evidence appearing real or future events already ruined. We thus need to understand both the factual and emotional basis of another's underlying fears and concerns related to divisive issues so that we can address these fears.

As is often stated, feelings are not facts. But they are real. Studies have shown that gut or instinctual feelings, more than facts and reasoning, underlie most people's strongly held beliefs.[1] Thus, consider asking probative questions concerning people's underlying anxieties, fears, and concerns and listening attentively to their responses. You may be able to find ways to alleviate any concerns.

If you believe a person's fears and concerns are based on inaccurate information or assumptions, providing corrective information may lead to a moderation of strongly held views and beliefs. However, because information is available from so many sources and channels today, much of it contested or unverified, be sensitive that conversations based heavily on perceived factual inaccuracies risk being counterproductive when not offered in a tactful or judicious manner.

Be willing to reexamine your own strongly held views— Be mindful of how your own limited or negative thinking or personal history can affect your views. If we want others to be open to at least considering our views, we, too, should be open to considering contrary ones and not judge or dismiss them outright. You may find parts you can agree on and work with. Remember, too, that your own unfounded or misplaced fears can impact your beliefs and views. Be willing to address their current validity. In doing so, you may find reasons for moderation or modification of your views and thus be able to reach some middle ground.

Acceptance Is a Choice

I understand your skepticism that acceptance conversations will help heal the Great Divide. I would be the first to admit that certain hard-core beliefs and issues have shown themselves to be so intractable, one-dimensional, and explosive that such conversations are ineffective, and people have little desire to have them.

But these conversations aren't always futile. If the people involved have a strong enough desire to try to make their lives and the world better, constructive and instructive conversations can take place. They are already occurring on a multitude of subjects and issues with the help of bridging organizations that are deeply concerned about the discord and acrimony among broad cross sections of our country.

Nonprofits such as Living Room Conversations, National Coalition for Dialogue and Deliberation, Listen First Project, and others are creating safe environments to foster listening, constructive dialogue, connection, and trust and understanding of one another.[2] These organizations typically offer structured formats for group conversations and dialogue and provide a wealth of helpful information, including conversation agreements, session guidelines, and best practices.

Constructive conversations are also occurring in many colleges and universities as part of their communication studies programs. Of particular note is Colorado State University's Center for Public Deliberation, which has had success in community problem-solving at the local level.[3]

I also understand that because many beliefs are deep and formed over many years, healing—particularly in the case of severe cultural, political, and family divisions—will likely be long and gradual, even with concerted efforts. But to me, that is not a reason to avoid such conversations, even if progress is slow and the conversations occur only among the few.

Let us bridge the "Space Between" by taking the chance—and risk—that the trust, understanding, and human connection that acceptance fosters will result in agreed facts and the discovery of communal space within the alternate universes. And no matter how small that space may initially be, the momentum, peace, and hope that acceptance creates will expand that space and help bridge the Great Divide.

I have repeatedly propounded that, fundamentally, acceptance is a choice we make. We can *all* choose acceptance and take steps to heal the Great Divide and abate the tidal wave that engulfs and threatens all our life currents.

INQUIRIES AND REFLECTIONS

- Do you believe the Great Divide can be lessened?
- What single steps are you willing to take to lessen it?
- Are you able to listen attentively to others with opposing views without dismissing or harshly judging them?
- Are you open to reexamining or moderating any of your own strongly held views?

The Waves Ahead

Dance with the waves, move with the sea, let the
rhythm of the water set your soul free.

—Christy Ann Martine

MY LIFE WITH THE Wave has recently come full circle. A
few years after being enthralled by the endless variety of
waves at the beach in Santa Monica, I went with a friend
to a Heal the Bay fundraiser in Malibu, known for its
beautiful beaches and surfable waves.

With over one hundred adults meandering around
at the event, my eyes were drawn to the marked contrast
of a lone woman dancing with some small children and
freely moving her body to the soothing sounds of a soulful blues singer. Although she was not my type (boy, was
I a limited thinker back then!), I was drawn to her easy,
flowing movements and soon found myself walking to
the dance area and dancing with the children close to her.

When the music stopped, we shared a few words,
and I thus began an unexpected, unplanned, uncharted,
and easy-flowing love wave with a beautiful (in all ways)
woman who lived in Santa Monica who quickly became
my type. Twenty-five years later, our love currents led to
the purchase of a small home in Malibu, where we are
blessed to wake up to the pulsating sounds and magnifi-
cence of ocean waves.

The way of the Wave has thus truly been my model
for navigating life's currents to destinations never before
reached or imagined. Although aligning with them

remains a work in progress for me, and always will, my rides continually improve through a greater awareness and understanding of how the obstructors disrupt the flow and how applying the mindsets and practices I've shared in the book significantly weakens their ripples. I hope that will be the case for you as well.

One of the challenges in countering the obstructors is an unawareness of their presence. They are often disguised beneath our frustrations, anxieties, worries, disappointments, resentments, impatience, and other heightened feelings and emotions—all clues that obstructors, particularly control, have invaded our waters and need addressing.

In your waves ahead, I encourage you to fully embrace the enhancers, especially trust and acceptance, as I strive to do. Your rides will be longer and smoother, and going with the flow will be easier and more natural.

I also encourage you to continually spend time in nature, even if for short durations or just going outdoors for a while. Nature embodies a natural rhythm, flow, and essence—one that is without the limitations, expectations, judgments, control, fear, and anger that easily undermine us.

Let nature be your model for a better life. Although waves are my model, there are others, such as tranquil forests, cascading falls, winding rivers, living deserts, and majestic mountains. Whatever model resonates with you, immerse and align yourself with the guidance, wisdom, and peace that nature offers.

May you go with the Wave!

Notes

Introduction

1. Oceanographers inform us that waves move energy, not water, and that the main factors in wave formation are gravitational forces, wind velocity, fetch (the distance wind can flow uninterrupted), and duration.

Chapter 1

1. Ralph Waldo Emerson, "Spiritual Laws," in *Essays, First Series* (Boston: Phillips, Sampson, 1857), 124–25.

Chapter 5

1. In *The Untethered Soul: The Journey Beyond* (Oakland, CA: New Harbinger, 2007), author Michael A. Singer explains the impact on us of this unrelenting inner critic in detail.
2. Kahlil Gibran, *Sand and Foam* (London: William Heinemann, 1927), 51.

Chapter 8

1. My wife has consented to including this story because of its potential to help others seeking recovery from their addictions.

Chapter 9

1. "God, grant me the serenity to accept the things I cannot change, courage to change the things I can, and wisdom to know the difference" (attributed to Reinhold Niebuhr, 1892–1971).

Chapter 11

1. Ralph Waldo Emerson, *May-Day and Other Pieces* (Boston: Ticknor and Fields, 1867), 186.
2. Seneca, *Oedipus*, ed. and trans. John C. Fitch in *Seneca: Tragedies II* (Cambridge, MA: Harvard University Press, 2018), 106–7.

Chapter 13

1. Jeff Greenwald, *The Best Tennis of Your Life: 50 Mental Strategies for Fearless Performance* (Cincinnati: Better Way Books, 2007), 110.

Chapter 16

1. Sri Daya Mata, *Intuition: Soul-Guidance for Life Decisions* (Los Angeles: Self-Realization Fellowship, 2003).

Chapter 17

1. I write about the ways that helped me let go of control in *Losing Control, Finding Serenity: How the Need to Control Hurts Us and How to Let It Go.*

Chapter 18

1. A poem I wrote and read at our wedding.
2. Thomas Merton, *No Man Is an Island* (Boston: Shambhala, 2005), 177–78.

Chapter 19

1. Mitchell Rosen, "Growth Is Key in Parent-Child Relationships," *Press-Enterprise*, October 18, 2014.
2. Kahlil Gibran, *The Prophet* (New York: Knopf, 1923), 21.

Chapter 20

1. "Perceived Control's Influence on Wellbeing in Residential Care versus Community Dwelling Older Adults," *Journal Happiness Studies* 15 (June 26, 2013): 845–55, doi.org/10.1007/s10902-013-9452-9.
2. "Can You Grow New Brain Cells?," Harvard Health Publishing, September 14, 2016, health.harvard.edu/mind-and-mood/can-you-grow-new-brain-cells; Lawrence Katz and Manning Rubin, *Keep Your Brain Alive: 83 Neurobic Exercises to Help Prevent Memory Loss and Increase Mental Fitness* (New York: Workman Publishing, 2014); and Lisa Armstrong, "Neurobic Tips: How to Exercise Your Brain," *She Knows*, October 8, 2013, sheknows.com/health-and-wellness/articles/1016375/neurobic-tips.

Chapter 21

1. Thomas Babington Macaulay, "John Dryden (January 1828)," in *The Miscellaneous Writings and Speeches of Lord Macaulay: Contributions to the Edinburgh Review, Vol. II* (London, 1871; Project Gutenberg, 2008), gutenberg.org/files/2168/2168h/2168-h.htm.
2. Learn more about Andrew Tischler's Painting Waves Tutorial at tischler.nz/painting-waves-tutorial/.

Chapter 22

1. Mike Digiovanna, "Albert Pujols Is No Longer Cause for Concern," *Los Angeles Times*, August 9, 2012.
2. Dylan Hernandez, "Adrian Gonzalez Sees Bright L.A. Future, Once He Fixes His Swing," *Los Angeles Times*, October 6, 2012.

Chapter 25

1. After the moratorium expired some months later, we were able to obtain legal possession of the space and re-leased it to a good

tenant at a higher rent. Although we retained the right to seek substantial past due rent, I elected not to.

Chapter 26

1. For more on the role of feelings and behavior, see Jonathan Haidt, *The Righteous Mind: Why Good People Are Divided by Politics and Religion* (New York: Pantheon, 2012).
2. For more on Living Room Conversations, visit livingroomconversations.org. For more on the National Coalition for Dialogue and Deliberation, visit ncdd.org /about.html. And for more on the Listen First Project, visit listenfirstproject.org/listen-first-coalition.
3. Visit https://cpd.colostate.edu to learn more about Colorado State University's Center for Public Deliberation.

Acknowledgments

I ALWAYS ASPIRED TO write and publish a book about the Wave after not publishing an earlier version I wrote over thirty-five years ago. At the time I was not aware of how much the obstructors impacted riding the Wave, nor did I know how to effectively counter them. I was also not aware of how much the enhancers influenced my going with the flow.

Simply put, I couldn't ride the Wave well enough myself, let alone explain how others could. That is why I am grateful to the people who were instrumental in helping me write this book. First and foremost, I want to thank my wife, life partner, and forever sweetheart, Sigute (who rides the Wave far better than me), for the key roles she played in the progression of the book: as the initial proofreader and editor; constructive, thoughtful critic; and loving supporter throughout the four-year writing journey.

The book has once again benefited greatly from a team of highly skilled and experienced writing and publishing professionals. Special thanks to Sharon Goldinger, my trusted and resourceful book consultant, who adeptly shepherded the book from its beginning to final publication, lending her remarkable "eye for details" in copyediting that enhanced the flow of the words.

I am grateful to Rabbi Beth Lieberman, for offering insightful content and organizational recommendations to make the way of the Wave clearer and more impactful, and to Mayapriya Long, for her skill and artistry in designing a book cover and interior layout that I feel captures the essence of the book, and for her kindness in providing me helpful feedback on an early manuscript of the book. I also want to thank David Greenwalt, for his suggestions about how to make the book more interesting to readers.

Thank you also to my three special children, Lana, Lora, and Brandon, for allowing me to share their instructive Wave-related stories, and in whom I take great pride and joy in witnessing how skillfully they navigate their own evolving life currents. And thank you to my sister, Suzee, for her love and continuous support of my writing endeavors.

In writing this book, I have been graced by, continually inspired by, and in awe of my amazing mother, Judy, who turned one hundred years of age as the final manuscript was finished in March 2024. My mother is truly an exemplar of navigating the inevitable challenges of elder currents in an accepting and graceful manner.

Finally, I am grateful to the Al-Anon program, whose guiding principles and practices have greatly enhanced my life currents, and to the members of its supportive fellowship for sharing their strength, hope, and experience.

About the Author

DANIEL A. MILLER, JD, is a writer, artist, poet, a nation-ally ranked seniors' master tennis player, and president of DM Properties, a privately owned real estate investment company.

He is the author of the best-selling *The Gifts of Acceptance*, a *Library Journal* 2018 Best Wellness Book of the Year, an IBPA Benjamin Franklin self-help and audiobook Silver Medal Winner, and a *Foreword Reviews* 2018 Book of the Year Award Finalist, and the best-selling *Losing Control, Finding Serenity*, a 2012 *Foreword Reviews* Book of the Year Award Finalist.

He graduated from UCLA with honors in business administration and finished in the top 5 percent of his class at the UCLA School of Law. While still in his twen-ties, he became a popular real estate instructor in the

UCLA extension program, and in his thirties he wrote a respected professional book, *How to Invest in Real Estate Syndicates*, and achieved financial success as a real estate investment advisor to the wealthy.

After suffering a series of traumatic events, Danny began a new journey, learning to surrender to the ups and downs of life. He now writes and speaks about the profound benefits of letting go of control, practicing acceptance, and navigating life's currents. His website features over 150 of his blog posts on control, acceptance, and flow dynamics and related subjects; his poetry; and his paintings.

He lives with his wife in Valley Village and Malibu, California. Danny welcomes your comments and invites you to contact him:

Website: danielamiller.com

Facebook: tinyurl.com/35fnmc9r

Library Journal Best Wellness Book of 2018,
IBPA Nonfiction Silver Winner, and
Foreword Reviews Book of the Year Award Finalist!

From the Best-Selling Author of
The Way of the Wave

THE GIFTS OF ACCEPTANCE
Embracing People and Things as They Are

Do you wish your parents had been more nurturing and supportive? Are you wondering if you'll ever find your ideal soul mate and dream boss? Do you wish you had perfect children, relatives who never fight, and friends who always agree with you?

No one gets to sail through life free of turbulence. What separates people who shake it off, bounce back, and stay positive from the bitter, never satisfied, and defeated?

Best-selling author and former compulsive controller Daniel A. Miller convincingly attests that the answer is choosing acceptance. In *The Gifts of Acceptance: Embracing People and Things as They Are*, Danny shares what he's learned—through extensive research, inspiring true stories, and his own experience with hardships—about the integral relationship between accepting the facts of life and others, with their quirks, flaws, and differences, and enjoying greater satisfaction in life.

Recognizing the benefits of acceptance isn't difficult. Yet the reality of accepting an unexpected job loss or financial setback, a friend's betrayal, a child's struggle with addiction, a serious illness, or even the annoying traits of a loved one can be extremely challenging. To make it easier, *The Gifts of Acceptance* offers insights, intentions, and strategies for practicing acceptance of parents, a significant other, children, siblings and extended family, coworkers, friends, and foes; of life's adversities and the limitations of getting older; and, perhaps toughest of all, of yourself.

You will learn how practicing acceptance helps you

- Navigate life's ups and downs more easily
- Enjoy greater trust, openness, and intimacy with your loved ones and those closest to you
- Survive control freaks, foes, and other crazy-makers
- Lift self-imposed burdens and obligations and experience less stress, frustration, and worry
- Reduce the struggle with your children
- Strengthen bonds with coworkers and business associates
- Discover new choices and opportunities in the most discouraging situations
- Turn setbacks and failures into future successes
- Find the path to secure self-acceptance

The Gifts of Acceptance is a book with the potential to repair relationships, revitalize careers, and make the world a better place.

Find out how accepting what is lets you discover what might be!

Get Your Copy Today!

The ebook can be purchased at Amazon.com (https://tinyurl.com/ms37p7hc) and Apple Books (https://tinyurl.com/cvcuvfeh).

The print book can be purchased at Amazon.com (https://tinyurl.com/3x5rbmje), at Barnesandnoble.com (https://tinyurl.com/yjj6y6f3), and through your favorite bookseller.